art and social function

art and social function

stephen willats

•••ellipsis

this edition published 2000 by
●●●ellipsis
www.ellipsis.com

first published 1976 by
latimer new dimensions limited

british library cataloguing in publication
a cip record for this book is available
from the british library

isbn 1 84166 053 1

printed in hong kong

●●●ellipsis is a registered trade mark of
ELLIPSIS LONDON LTD
2 rufus street, london n1 6pe

contents

audience and authorship

The realisation that all 'art' is dependent on society – dependent on the relationships between people and not the sole product of any one person – is becoming increasingly important in the shaping of future culture. This divestment of authorship is seen as more relevant to an emerging culture founded on networks of exchange, fluidity, transience, and mutuality, as it ultimately offers us the prospect of self-organisation in personal and interpersonal society.

However, the origination of the models and conceptions that are shaping our contemporary communication-driven society grew out of the interdisciplinary exchanges of the 1950s and early 1960s. These mapped out the philosophical and technological foundations of dynamic, responsive decision-making systems, and processes of exchange, learning and adaption.

In the late 1950s I responded to this new climate and reacted against what I saw as the determinism of 'art' at the time. I made the basic observation that the audience was as important as the artist in the origination and reception of a work of art, and moreover that the artwork was a potential vehicle of exchange between the two. While I was working at an avant-garde art gallery in London during 1958–59 I noticed that the 'audience' went there to look for icons of certainty, icons which were the verified ideal projections of society, and which had an emulative and authoritative role in the formation of consciousness. Culture was in the role of providing psychological certainty – past, present, future. I wondered what would happen if the audience found only uncertainty, even confronted chaos or a random variable inside the art gallery, but was given the tools and the possibility of intervening to express creatively their own order, their own certainty, arrived at personally. My reasoning was that this actual personal creative experience would be more meaningful to people than their innate position as passive witnesses to referential experience in the traditional audience role. These factors led me to redefine the whole idea of both 'audience' and 'art institution', making them central to the work's conception.

By 1965 I had begun to map out what was then a completely new physical and social territory for an artwork to operate within. I saw the artwork as a dynamic structure of events in time, dependent on exchanges between people, reflecting their inherent relativity in perception, being tied to a context that was already meaningful to those people. The artwork was seen as operating within the domain of the 'audience', using their language and priorities, etc. This was very much in the spirit of opening up the demarcated boundaries between separated disciplines which typified thinking. This climate enabled me to go far beyond the existing framework of 'art', and explore the possibilities for strategies in communication found in cybernetics, advertising, social sciences, information theory, and so on. These explorations led to strategies employed in the works discussed later in this book. They owed little or nothing to the firmly rooted precedents in art – this was genuine virgin territory.

In the origination and presentation of these works was the excitement and uncertainty of knowing that no one had tried anything quite like this before. Thus, from my experiments on a housing estate on the outskirts of Ipswich in

1965 to the West London Social Resource Project in 1972, there was a trial-and-error process of trying to realise and manifest conceptual models into the pragmatic of actuality.

The creation of precedent that was required for this to happen, and the necessary accompanying change of mind-set, led me to think of *Art and Social Function* as a kind of manual or tool that would be relevant to any artist thinking of enacting different paradigms for an art intervening in the fabric of society. The value of this book would be that it was the personal testament of an artist's experiences, offered to others to draw upon and, in this respect, it was unusual in its formulation, for within the art domain the discussion about the merits of art practice is usually considered the preserve of the art critic or historian.

By the time the book was originally published in 1976, the works discussed in its texts had already led on to *From A Coded World*, Perivale, West London, 1975, and *Vertical Living*, Hayes, West London, 1976, which further extended and refined the approach.[1, 2] In fact the ideas expressed in *Art and Social Function* have informed a progression of works up to the present; for example Meta Filter directly leads to the interactive simulations Freezone (1997) and Creativeforce (1998).[3, 4]

Artists concerned about the future of art practice, its function and meaning and its possible relevance to the present and future social setting, will find that many of the issues they will undoubtedly face are examined here in *Art and Social Function*. The three works which are discussed at length demonstrated that the social and physical domain within which art operates could in reality extend well beyond the given territory legitimised by the institutions of art for operation, and could find meaningful ways of functioning within the daily fabric of people's lives. But to take this large step, the very foundations of thinking that characterise art within the museum have to be abandoned and a new framework built that encompasses the change of context and network of exchange. This is still and importantly true – more so in many ways – as interactive technologies increasingly influence the way we think and live. And so I think that this republication of *Art and Social Function* will be found interesting and useful by those initiating new practice in art now.

Stephen Willats, April 2000

1 Stephen Willats, 'Between a Symbolic World and a Contextual Reality: The Artwork as a Vehicle for Forwarding Counter-Consciousness', *Control* Magazine 10, November 1977, page 13.
2 Stephen Willats, 'The Counter Consciousness In Vertical Living', *Control* Magazine 11, November 1979, page 4.
3 Stephen Willats, 'Freezone', in *The Artwork as Interactive Simulation*, The Mappin Art Gallery, Sheffield, 1998, page 28.
4 Stephen Willats, 'Creativeforce', in *The Artwork as Interactive Simulation*, page 33.

introduction

In common with other areas of activity, art practice operates within an environment of institutions and groups of people which effectively maintain it as an identifiable activity within society. This defines what can be called the territory of art in society, and I shall refer to it as 'art's social environment'.[1] The artist, in operating within the delineated territory of 'art's social environment', has largely restricted the area of function of art practice to its internal fabric of norms and conventions. Within such contained conditions the artist has been able to develop methods for communicating intentional concepts to a largely predictable audience, in that they have tended to be the other members of 'art's social environment' (see figure 1).[2] The audience's prior knowledge of art enables the artist to use a predictive language as a 'restricted code'. A 'restricted code' can be simply defined as a coding structure linked to a particular social/geographical context, relying as a means of communication on people acquiring or learning the associative links the code has within a defined world.[3]

It is up to the audience to predict the associative links made by the artist that enable him to indulge in increasingly abstract and less available language requiring prior knowledge to successfully gain access to the work's intent. In a similar fashion, the artist's conception/work has – in the absence of any overriding criteria for art within society – become increasingly concerned with what is immediately meaningful within the contained social environment in which he operates. What has seemed meaningful are the conventions of art's social environment; as a result this has become a major preoccupation of much contemporary art, overriding an involvement with any wider intentional subject matter. Artists, in attempting to initiate a reordering in audience perception, generally limit their activity to changing the way the activity 'art' is seen, such concerns predominating as what constitutes an artwork, and how one should behave with regard to it within art's institutions. If, as has already been suggested, an audience is comprised of members of 'art's social environment', the artist is 'preaching to the converted'. If however, he addresses an audience from outside this community then what he postulates is likely to be far removed from the audience's existing priorities. This situation reinforces the state of separateness which exists between the orientations of art practice and of society in general. The essentially self-referential nature of art practice has rendered it imprisoned by its own framework, and this has effectively prevented it from spreading the understanding of its concerns, or widening its audience beyond the boundaries of its own social environment.

Art of course does function to a degree beyond its own social territory; the criteria used here however is whether work functions as a means of communication to an audience in accordance with what the artist envisaged. In examining the criteria by which the artist functions in modern society, information from other disciplines concerned with problems of communication (such as cybernetics) can be relevant.[4] This may require not only a redefinition of what constitutes an artwork but also a widening of the context in which artworks are presented. In order to achieve this, the artist will need to direct his intentional concerns towards what is meaningful in a wider social context. This will require the development of methodologies appropriate to what a wider audience perceives as meaningful, which in turn leads to the position expressed here concerning the relative and context-dependent nature of people's cognition.[5] Two people viewing the same x might refer to different worlds of YS. However, underlying these differences in the cognition of the worlds of YS are common structures in the form of parameters which determine their formation. A parameter is considered here to be a fundamental set of rules that underlies a system. Stemming from a parameter is a derivative structure that determines the various external forms a system takes. Thus, though the way in which one person might greet another might vary from context to context, the action of greeting functions as a parameter from which various forms of coded greeting behaviour are derived.

An area of attention which is particularly pertinent to the prescriptive function of art practice concerns the underlying parameters of social behaviour and as such this has an implicative structure that extends the artist's conceptions directly into society. The artist forwards prescriptive conceptualisations that concern relationships between parameters underlying different social behaviours and their derivative coding structures. These codings are a formalisation of the conventions and norms within society. The way in which they manifest themselves reflects the nature of relationships existing in different contexts. The artist, in forwarding a prescriptive view of these coding structures, reorders the audience's perception of its own behaviour, so that it is able to relate a presented situation to a social parameter. From this the audience can contextualise the inferences made within an already articulated world of references. Thus the audience relates the parameter's derivative structure to its own frame of reference. As a result, the audience is able to make inferences to similar structures more readily than it could from the parameter's context-dependent derivatives, i.e. coding structures. In this way the artist directly uses the audience's world of references and as a result is able to widen considerably the composition of his audience. Instead of presenting a preferred view, i.e. presuming that the artist's views will be seen as meaningful by his audience, the artist embraces the concept of pluralism and accepts the relativity of the audience's perception and the context-dependency of his work. The artist directs the audience's attention towards a given view, and provides the means to examine it in a particular way, but does not prescribe specific meaning that should be brought to bear on it. Instead the audience experiences the work and searches for new meanings from within the realm of what is already meaningful.

the west london social resource project

background model

The conception of the West London Social Resource Project took place during March 1972 and was based on two earlier works initiated during 1971, entitled 'Man from the Twenty First Century Project', and the 'Social Resource Project for Tennis Clubs'. These were attempts to extend not only the concerns of art practice, but also the social territory in which it functioned. They were somewhat optimistic in what they set out to achieve, and were consequently never fully realised, though they did provide the conceptual area of attention, and the basis of methodologies for later works. As they were very much pilot works for what was to follow, I have provided a brief description of each in references 6 and 7. The fundamental concern of all of these, and the two later ones, was the relationship between coding structures and patterns of behaviour.

Coding structures have an important role in formalising internal relationships within social groupings. The establishment of formal relationships between people is fundamental to any social organisation, or grouping, and from this develops a structure of behaviour conventions which govern interaction within that grouping. These conventions form a parameter that underlies the grouping and becomes the criteria for membership of it. The form that conventions or norms take reflects, and also reinforces, the aspirations, motivations, and level of organisation of the group. In this sense, the way people code themselves (how they dress, how they speak) or their home environment (the front garden, living room, the kind of car they own) can reflect their desired or actual position within a community. I have called the externalised manifestation of this process, 'life codes'. The basis of conventions that influence interpersonal behaviour is conditioned by the internal models one person constructs of another from life codes, which affect his perception of the other person. A model is defined as a set of interconnected representations that are used to illustrate the state of a more complex structure. Thus a model is a symbolic structure which is used to pare down the real world into a form that expresses its essence. In this sense a model differs from a replica, which consists of a duplication of an original, even though on a different scale. I have used the word 'model' here to refer to a person's mental representations which have been formalised into a structure, whose features correspond to another structure.

The basic elements in building up perceptions of other people have been called intent-act-effect units. These units are used to organise our internal representations of other people's behaviour into models. In other words we go beyond observable coding of behaviour, and make casual inferences as to why the behaviour occurred, or what the codings specify in terms of a person's subsequent actions, i.e. their motivations, aspirations etc. Thus, in forming a response to another person, reference is made to an implicitly held structure of representations acting as guidelines to what his codings signify. Other variables such as context and identity must also affect the inferences between the intent-act-effect units. For example, if the identity of a person was a friend, and the context afternoon tea at home, his actions would be more likely to be perceived as warm than cold. 'Warm' would in turn imply generous rather than mean. If a person is a stranger and already seen as cold, then there is little trouble in seeing him as aggressive, and so on. The model that we form of a particular individual is derived from an internally held matrix of correlated traits or characteristics. Within this matrix, some characteristics are closer to each other than others. These relationships tend to exist in categories: reference to one within a particular category tends to direct the subsequent nature of inferences made in constructing the component parts of a model. Having selected 'cold', we are more likely to find 'mean' than 'generous'; in fact the latter could be seen as conflicting. The construction of models by a person is a central feature in his search for actions that will enable him to maintain an ordered, stable relationship with his environment, both social and physical. The construction of a model from past behaviour within the environment enables the person to predict its present state, which is necessary if he is to exercise control over it.

In discussing models it is useful to divide them into three different classes (though in reality they would be interdependent). The three classes of models are: descriptive models, which depict the present state of a structure; predictive models, which depict the probable state of a structure; prescriptive models, which depict the possible state of a structure. While descriptive models can be used as a foundation for the constructions of predictive models or vice versa, they can both act as a heuristic (in this sense, a piece of previously acquired information which is used as a guide for solving future problems) in the construction of prescriptive models. Within a social organisation such as a neighbourhood social group, the implicit models a person holds of his relationship to other members is conditional on the foundation of normative beliefs generated within that context. Code structures provide formal criteria for the externalisation and reinforcement of internal representations and through a person's response new models are formed. These models would fall within the categories outlined earlier; for example, it would be essential for an individual to construct predictive models to make rational decisions about future actions. On the other hand prescriptive models generated within a social organisation imply a possibility of change in the foundation of beliefs among its membership.

The internal structure of a social group is organised around fundamental drives that act as underlying parameters. One of these drives which affects the composition of a social group, and is perhaps the most important factor in maintaining its identity, is the drive towards social stability.[8] The drive towards stability results in pressure from the group on the individual to 'conform'. 'Group pressure is a psychological force operating upon a person to fulfil others' expectations of him including especially those expectations of others relating to the person's "roles" or to behaviours specified or implied by the "norms" of the group to which he belongs ... The need for a member to be accepted by other members of the group to which he aspires, causes him to seek to reduce potential conflicts by agreeing or at least seeming to agree with attitudes and behaviour norms of other members. In seeming to agree a person is complying with a group's norms, though if he envisages himself as a fully integrated member then the beliefs of the group will have to be acquired through their private acceptance.' Kiesler and Kiesler make a distinction between private acceptance of group norms, and compliance with those norms; while the pressure from the group on an individual would be towards private acceptance, compliance might well be tolerated within certain situations, especially those involving more public forms of behaviour.

The importance of stability for a group's survival can be appreciated when it is considered that it is in a stable state that an organisation can best construct a predictive model of its environment.[9] The structure of norms and conventions of a social group plays an important part in the drive towards stability. Norms provide a means of reference for a group's membership, and the display of appropriate codings is an important preoccupation of members in maintaining cohesiveness and group identity. For example, it would be difficult for someone wearing a pinstriped suit, bowler hat, umbrella and carnation to enter a class of art students and to be accepted as part of the same community. Similarly what I have termed 'social resources'[10] have a considerable role in reinforcing behaviour norms and coding within a group. There are a wide variety of social resources, coming in many different forms, for example, clubs, community centres, football on a Saturday afternoon, tea break at work, Boy Scouts, Sunday morning church. The form they take depends on the social group. For instance, at one level you can think of a tennis club as being centred around tennis as a sport, but it also serves what might be considered a more important function within a particular social group by satisfying certain other needs:

1 it reaffirms, and strengthens their social group's attitudes, coding structures, etc. through casual contact between

members;
2 it enables power and dominance drives to be fulfilled at a ritualistic level.

In discussing group behaviour, a distinction should be made between conventions, coding norms, etc., that are generated by the group themselves, and those acquired from sources external to the group. In the latter case these conventions and coding norms are adhered to in order to conform as individuals, and as a group, to projectional stereotypes generated in society. These projectional stereotypes are held as life codes which embody ideal values, and are forwarded as such to be emulated. For example, though a middle-class group might evolve its own codes, these are in general a variation on a projectional stereotype which affects the way they dress, the way they live and so on, and would distinguish them from the membership of another social group. Various mechanisms such as advertising or magazines, have acquired the function of generating projectional stereotypes within social groups.

Another aspect of the background to the West London Social Resource Project concerned decision-making models, and especially their effect on social groupings. A typical model of decision making within organisations that are predominantly geared to making decisions would in essence be similar to the decision role model in figure 2. This model illustrates a system where groups of people have different decision-making roles. People in operational research such as Stafford Beer[11] are postulating new decision-making models which in some cases bear little relation to my decision role model.

The system that I have depicted is hierarchical. The apex

consists of an orienting body made up of a comparatively small number of contributing members, compared to the number of members in the rest of the system. The orienting body acts as a control over the system in that it provides the constraints for the rest of the structure. The orienting body feeds decisions of a directional nature to a decision tree, which formalises the information it receives into a more detailed form, ready for instructing those who will carry out the decisions. The flow of information through the decision tree is essentially unidirectional, from layer to layer, each level relying on precedents prescribed from higher levels in the tree. The decision tree in turn feeds what I have defined as a machine base, so-called because of the small amount of decision-making associated with it. The machine base implements the decisions that are prescribed to it from the decision tree.

In the West London Project various social groupings were linked to my decision role map, as a means of distinguishing between them, and of delineating their social territories. In making these classifications a distinction could be made between an area manager of a group of shops, the manager of one of these shops, and the people who were employed behind the counter. Around these decision-making roles, groups formed, and the social territory of these groups was largely delineated by their relative position to each other in my model. These classifications were convenient for conceiving the structure of the project, and were not referred to in any way during its operation. In this sense the interpersonal structures of neighbourhood social groupings provided the general setting for the West London Project, and my map of decision roles was used to identify the particular context in which it functioned.

the notion of an optimum model

The methods employed in the projects described in this book were to a large extent developed as a result of a critical assessment of the performance of traditional methods of communicating intentional concerns to a wider audience. The basis of these methods was arrived at with recourse to research material from technologies of communication and theories of learning, and I shall now briefly outline some of their principle features.[12] As a result of examining methods in a pragmatic fashion a procedure was evolved for a work of art that involved three determining factors:

1 the intentions of the artist;
2 the social/geographical context in which the work would be forwarded; and
3 the audience to which the work would be presented.[13]

These variables had to be decided upon before considering the form the work would take. The form of the work would then result from the best balance that could be achieved between all three factors. These requirements thus formed the basis of a pragmatic approach towards methodologies, and gave rise to what I have termed an optimum model.[14] As a methodological concept the optimum model reflects ideas developed in philosophical cybernetics. Central to it is the principle of feedback whereby a system arrives at a state of organisation through a series of interactions with external variables, upon which it depends in some way. The system continually evolves according to the balance between inputs from external variables and outputs in the form of responses to those variables, until it reaches equilibrium. In formulating methodologies for an optimum model the artist would function in a similar way with the three determining factors acting as the dependent variables.

some theoretical features of an optimising approach

There are numerous ways in which a person acquires his perception of events or phenomena:

1 an external source transmits information to him which subsequently affects his perception, A tells B about X; and
2 he experiences the events or phenomena directly, A sees X.

Although we all acquire information by both means, the latter will almost certainly be the most effective. This is because transmitted information, as far as the receiver is concerned, deals with referential experience which is not as meaningful as direct interaction with the perceived object/ event.

In using task-oriented methods the projects forwarded a model representing a process consisting of a number of tasks structured into a sequence. The participant was presented initially with concepts involving aspects of the world which were already familiar to him and gradually progressed to more difficult and less familiar conceptual territory. In completing a sequence of tasks a person activated a model, in so far as a model is a dynamic process. Clearly the nature of the tasks had to be related to the environment in which they were to take place.

In their book *Human Problem Solving* Simon and Newell outline these conditions as a task environment, an environment coupled with a goal, problem or task.[15] In talking about a task environment they suggest that we distinguish carefully between the environment itself, the participant's perception of that environment and the theorist's perception of that environment. This is in keeping with the optimum model approach; the task environment represents the second factor as outlined above. It is obvious that the artist will need to do a certain amount of reconnaissance before methods or tasks are to be developed if he is to define the task environment and the perception of it by his intended participants. In devising tasks he will need to ensure that the tasks are neither so near to the participants' existing comprehension of the environment as to appear normative nor so far removed as to seem unconnected and perhaps meaningless. The objective should be a middle point between these two polarities so that the tasks can be seen to be sufficiently different within the task environment to stimulate participation but not so different that there would be too few references for it to be seen as relevant. In ascertaining the participant's perceptions of the task environment, reference would also need to be made to the language with which they articulate these perceptions. Knowledge of this would be useful in coding the tasks in that the use of the participants' existing language would remove, to some degree, the need for them to acquire a new language before they begin the project. The context used to represent the task environment and the language used to code the tasks should not be seen as two independent conditions for both rely on participant acceptance. The siting of the task environment within a context that is readily understood by participants and the use of a language to which they have easy access will facilitate such acceptance.[16] Such a context was found to be their home environment. If the artist uses the participant's home as the task environment he needs to ascertain the special associative meanings attached to language by participants in that environment. These languages are referred to by Basil Bernstein as 'restricted codes'.[17]

In structuring tasks into a sequence a system is in effect set up which is similar to involving participants in a process of learning as they establish their own way to complete these tasks. In establishing the situation in which learning can occur, it is vital to specify a goal which is shared by both the programmer of such conditions – in this case the artist – and the subject – the participant. This is important not only to motivate the participant to begin the task sequence, but also to maintain his involvement. The loss of sight of the specified goal by a participant would in all likelihood mean either reversing his progression in the learning sequence, or unlearning what he has learnt, or simply transferring his attention elsewhere. The nature of the goal is as important as its continual perception in creating motivation. The recognition of some part of it as relevant to an existing need will increase its meaningfulness and thus help to create impetus towards its attainment. But there is no reason why a goal should be seen as immediately meaningful if it is understood to be part of a wider goal, attained by way of sub-routines. These sub-routines would inevitably have their own sub-goals and would be structured into a sequence that was initially based on existing priorities, only varying from them gradually when sustained participation had been obtained. If the sub-routines were each seen as individual elements of the wider goal then, as they were achieved, so that wider goal would gradually be revealed.

Here we begin to get a picture of the kind of methods that were seen as appropriate to the notion of an optimum model as used in the projects. We have the idea that the artist's intentional model is formed into a sequence of states with which a person interacts over a period of time. The sequence is directed towards a person attaining an objective – a goal – which they were able to recognise as related to their existing priorities. The sequence of states is made up of a number of tasks which in themselves represent sub-routines on the path towards the goal. In completing one of these, a person realises part of the goal.[18] In structuring sub-routines into a sequence, some tasks would be more difficult to accomplish than others, especially those relying on some prior knowledge. In this case the sub-routines would need to be graduated according to the knowledge required to accomplish them. For example, in a learning sub-routine with dependent tasks 1 to 6, 1 would be the least difficult, 2 the next; and so on until 6, which would be the most difficult. The accomplishment of task 6 would be dependent on the retention of learnt information from 1 to 5. If task 6 was presented as task 1, a participant would be left with insufficient information or skill to accomplish it, and this could result in him giving up the attempt. Sequencing can be achieved by providing a mechanism which controls, through feedback, the relationships between the tasks encountered and the participant's ability to complete them. The mechanism could present tasks to a participant in the form of problems requiring completion by a search through his own experiences, and transferring them as a heuristic.[19] Problems would be open-ended, a participant being able to supply a solution in the way he found most relevant. In a structured sequence of tasks, the problems would point to an area of attention forming some aspect of the artist's intention. The full concept would not become apparent to a participant until he had solved a number of the problems. Problems expressed in question form are especially useful in this context in that they tend to force participants to formulate explicitly, internal representations held implicitly.[20] McKay points out that in asking a question, a person is expressing a state of uncertainty, or a state of unreadiness to interact purposefully with the world around him, and more specifically with the person the question is directed towards. In other words the questioner has an incomplete picture of the world, and therefore directs a question towards the area of incompleteness. In answering a question, a person is attempting to complete the questioner's picture of that area of uncertainty, and this requires him to order his own understanding into a form that can be readily understood by the questioner.

the conception of the project

In laying the foundation for what was to become the West London Project,[21] reference to the concept of a social resource had quite a different emphasis than that of the Tennis Project, and this involved the notion of an artwork functioning as a social resource in its own right. While art as an activity has functioned as a resource for particular social groupings, this has generally, within recent history, been incidental to the intention of the artist. The West London Project postulated the notion of an artwork as a social resource operating outside institutions dedicated to art, as an integral part of its audience's daily routines. In this sense an artwork functions as an integral feature of the environment in which a person lives, and is regarded as such by him.

The reason for envisaging an artwork as a social resource was tied to the practicalities of widening the social territory of art practice by centring the area of communication outside the art community to involve an audience who were likely to have little knowledge or interest in fine art. The use of art institutions was obviously inappropriate to a non art-oriented audience. A work that itself took the form of a social resource could function as its own institution and could encompass a wide range of coding behaviours. In specifying an audience outside art's social environment two basic conditions had to be carefully considered. The first of these considerations involved the composition of the audience, and stemming from this the selection of the environment for the work. These two decisions were so important to successful communication that, after a coherent intentional concept for the work had been formed, the audience composition and the work's environment had to be decided before the methods used to construct the work were devised. This was further reinforced by the actual objectives of the project which were concerned with the way different groups of people coded their lives. The audience decided upon was four groups of people, representing four different, though typical, life codes.

In selecting who the groups should include reference was made to my decision role model, so that each group would be a well-defined social group. From this four social groups emerged that were initially defined as upper middle class, middle middle class, lower middle class, and working class. These classifications were really only useful in providing a way of making distinctions between the groups when the project was conceived in its abstract form. When the audience groups were actually selected, the criteria used was that the groups should see themselves as typical and as different or separate from the other social groups. It was decided to centre the project on the geographical area of outer west London, and to find within its boundaries the four social groups. In the project's embryonic stages it could have equally made use of any other geographical area of any other town or city that contained a number of distinctly different social groupings. A number of reconnaissance trips were made into west London with a photographer, to ascertain suitable locations for the project (see figure 3).

This research type of activity represented a distinct departure from traditional methods in art, and by the time this work had finished, the form the project was to take owed little to previous or existing art practice. The reconnaissance mainly centred on the Hayes, Greenford, Hanwell, Osterley, Northolt districts, and while driving around taking photographs of suitable areas, we noticed tracts of scrubland used largely as unofficial rubbish dumps generally between the housing estates in areas such as Hayes and parts of Northolt. It seemed as though these were waste lands between communities, and I adopted the term 'West London Waste Lands' as a project slogan (see figure 4). I felt that people would recognise this slogan, as indeed they did, as referring to a particular physical feature of their environment to which they could attach some special meaning, and this would then facilitate their acceptance of the project.

During the reconnaissance trips, photographs forming a general survey of the districts were taken, and used in the selection of the four groups. Having decided on the likely general locations in west London for the project, a more specific search was made within those locations for suitable sites. A site was selected if it was considered to be a homogeneous representation of one of the typical social groups. It was felt that such homogeneity was more likely to be found within residential neighbourhoods, and, as a result, a search was made for a small number of streets that were interconnected to form an obvious delineated area. Figures 5 and 6 show the relationship of the project areas to their surrounding districts, and to each other. They tend to form a line across west London connected by a number of roads running into each other, forming a route that links them together. Having settled on the composition of the project's audience and its environment, the shape that it was to take now began to emerge. The project was seen as taking the form of a prescriptive model. The area of attention that the model was given was directed towards the way people code their environment as extensions and reinforcements of their aspirations. This personal environment encompasses the interior of a person's house, garden, selection of transport methods, style of dress, etc.

The objective of the project was to show the people who took part in it the role of behaviour conventions in determining the nature of coding structures, and subsequently how these structures affected the formation of people's attitudes, and perceptions of their immediate environment. The intention was that by making analogies from the project's prescriptive model, people could increase their awareness of their own life codes and other people's, and the role that they had within everyday routines related to their neighbourhood. It was thought this would increase understanding within the community of people's needs for coding that environment, and that people would remodel their representations of coding structures in accordance with those needs.

It should be stressed that the project was seen as a neutral tool in the sense that, though it was to draw people's attention to specific parts of their environment, it was not intended to dictate to them a particular way in which it should be perceived. The project was not seen as a static model, but as a dynamic one in the form of an interactive learning system which would be operational as a process through time (see figure 7). The audience would not view this process as they would view an object but they would become participants, and its operation was dependent on their involvement. As a process the project was divided into a number of parts, so that a person could gradually gain access into the work's concerns. These parts were interrelated to form a sequence that changed from descriptive modelling to prescriptive modelling. In other words, the first part of the project involved a participant's perception of how he saw his environment and the latter parts how it possibly could or should be. This sequence was finally to terminate at a point where participants developed a consensus model drawn from all four project areas. This sequence, from which the interactive learning system was constructed, employed different forms of task-oriented methods to enable participants to contextualise the work's various concerns. In order to obtain involvement from non art-oriented persons the project would need to operate as closely as possible to their existing priorities, and to require at least initially very little in the way of any divergence from normal routines. It was considered to be inappropriate to use an art-based coding language; instead it was decided to use references drawn from participants' own neighbourhoods as far as possible.

the initiation of the project

The project operators included a photographer, a cybernetician and a sociologist, but the main fieldwork was done by a team which I called the West London Super Girls. This team had the function of introducing the project to the residents of the four project areas, and inviting them to participate. A number of ways of initiating the project had been considered (including leafletting and newspaper advertising), but in the end it was decided that a person-to-person approach was by far the best, as it was interactive and inherently the most flexible, for if a person did not understand something then he could ask a question. A lot hinged on the initial contact with potential participants, and we thought it would facilitate a more favourable response if project operators dressed and spoke in a similar way to the people who were being invited to participate. The importance of visual presentation had been noted in the 'Man from the Twenty First Century Project' where an art student who had dressed in a similar fashion to the people he was interviewing had a better response, in terms of people agreeing to fill in a questionnaire and subsequently doing so, than art students who just presented themselves as themselves. I therefore tried to build up a team of West London Super Girls by standing in various high streets in west London, and recruiting from those who responded to a leaflet. The substance of this is reproduced in figure 8.

From the response to the leaflets and through friends, a team of six was arrived at. It is interesting to note that the West London Super Girls were much more successful than a similar male team in obtaining co-operation from potential participants. The project was introduced to residents of the project areas by project operators calling from door to door[22] and undertaking the following procedure. After the door had been opened, the project operators gave a simple account of the project, taking care to mention in the initial sentences that the project was an artwork. If the potential participant seemed interested at this stage, the project operators then went into detail about what was involved in participating and then finally asked them whether they would like to take part.

The structure of the doorstep introduction to the project was arrived at after a number of trials, where different things that had to be said were tried in various orders. From these trials it was ascertained that it was important to mention the relationship of the project to art straight away, and to ask whether the resident would like to participate after about three minutes' discussion. It was found that the more information a person had, the more certain he would feel about taking part. The first observation was caused by what could well be called 'doorstep inhibition'. As soon as the resident opened the front door, and saw two of the project operators standing there (it was also found important for two project operators to go together, one acting as a support for the other), he or she started to construct a response that might initially concern the project operators' appearance in simple terms of desirable or undesirable. This would then be elaborated to involve probable motives and effects; for instance, they were from the council, the local church, or a political party, they were salesmen, etc. These anticipatory responses, if allowed to build up, would have inhibited the successful outcome of the discussion, and people were generally more co-operative when their initial reaction was shown to be wrong. Later on in the project people made plain that many of them – a large majority of participants – would not have taken part if the project had been connected to any of the previously mentioned categories. For all these categories people had some form of prior association, while the majority had only distant notions about art but were ready to consider what must have seemed quite a radical deviation from their experience, as it was presented as concerning them directly. In the few cases where people already had a model of art constructed from some form of personal involvement, the response was a strong negative. This was because they tried to integrate the project within their own terms of reference for art, and were therefore not able to comprehend the project as an artwork at all. The people who responded in this way were an amateur painter, an art teacher at a local school and a collector of racing paintings.

Project operators went from door to door in the streets within the project areas, and on average they spent about five minutes with each person they spoke to. This includes the time spent answering people's questions about the project. One factor that must inevitably have helped in getting a co-operative response was that project operators made it quite clear that a participant's identity would remain anonymous. Neither a person's name nor their house number was revealed publicly anywhere in the project, and project operators did not even ask their name.

Before the project started we estimated that about 30 participants would be required from each project area. On average about one in two of the people who were invited to participate said that they would like to do so. Thus of 210 people asked, 109 agreed to take part. This was in fact initially a provisional agreement; it was arranged that project operators would call back one week later to see if people still wanted to participate. During the participant-gathering stage of the project, all the project operators were concentrated in one project area at a time, and they moved from area to area, after the required number of participants had been obtained. It was essential to the project that all participants should start together, and the gap between the two interviews provided a convenient period of time for project operators to switch from area to area. Also the two preliminary meetings reduced the number of people who might drop out of the project early on, by giving them time to think about what was entailed in taking part, as well as eliminating those who said they would participate as a way of terminating the front door discussion.

After the second discussion the number of participants was reduced to 79, with 17 in area one, 23 in area two, 20 in area three and 19 in area four. Before the project started, I went to Hounslow Libraries Department to discuss the use of Osterley library at a later stage of the project, and was told that various schemes had been tried in the district of project area three, but that these had always obtained an extremely low response in terms of people's co-operation and interest. Also other artists and sociologist friends who had tried to obtain co-operative responses from the general public indicated from their experiences that a low response should be expected. It is interesting to bear these comments in mind when considering responses to the project.

tasks of participants in the first stage of the project

A person effectively started to participate in the project as soon as he had agreed to take part during the initial doorstep introduction. Having done so the new participant was given a leaflet on the project (figure 9) and a window poster (figure 10). These two items were seen as having an important role in getting the project operating during the period between the first and second introductory meetings, and in this respect they fulfilled two interconnected functions. The first of these functions was to reinforce, and thus maintain, participants' involvement in the project which might otherwise be dissipated in the interim period between the two introductory meetings. The second function was to spread knowledge of the project among residents in the project areas, and generally create interest in it, and thus help to increase its acceptability. We found that if a person had prior knowledge of the project, which had been acquired by word of mouth, he was much more likely to agree to participate. The act of agreeing to participate and of telling another person about the project would also reinforce the participant's personal commitment.

This form of neighbourhood interaction was facilitated by the leaflets, and one was specially designed for each project area. A project area's leaflet had reproduced on it items taken from its neighbourhood which participants were likely to be familiar with, as they were with the title, 'West London Waste Lands'. People's recognition of the reproduced neighbourhood items became almost a game in itself, and generated considerable response, especially if they knew the owner of the depicted item, or it was their own. The window posters were intended to have the same function as the project area leaflets; in practice they did not have the same impact. When the project was conceived each participant was to receive a number to be entered in a space provided on the window poster, and they were supposed to stick a photograph of themselves on it, before displaying it on their front window. Only about one in three participants displayed the posters, and all except one did so without the photograph of themselves. By the middle stages of the project (after five months) all of the posters had been removed. However, enough window posters were displayed, without portraits, for them to make an initial visual impact in the project areas. There is no doubt that the publicity material led some participants to become acquainted for the first time even though they had been close neighbours for a long time.

During the second visit by the project operators, participants who wanted to continue were given a copy of the West London Manual (see figure 11). The manual was the main tool to be used by participants in the first stage of the project, and had been specially designed to externalise a participant's internal descriptive representations of coding structures and behaviour conventions within their physical and social environment. The manual, which was given to each participant as a task to be completed, comprised a series of problems, mostly in the form of open questions. Each individual problem formed part of a sequence of problems designed to facilitate the externalisation of a participant's representation of a particular part of his environment. The manual was formulated so that as a participant progressed through the sequence of problems he would gradually assemble elements until a complete picture was obtained. The manual contained 60 problems in all, which participants worked through in sequence: however, they had been told that they need not complete all the problems.

The sequence of problems was in two main sections. The first provided an initial access to the concerns of the project, by familiarising participants with the process of externalisation. This set of problems was divided into a number of subsections, the first of these being designed to introduce the participant to the methodology. To do so, participants were instructed to identify from a page of reproduced incomplete objects taken from the project areas, the complete scene presented on two adjoining sheets. Having entered their answer into the manual, they were then asked to describe the associations they felt they had with the completed object. In the second subsection a participant progressed to problems that asked specific questions about particular neighbourhood items, and this began to direct a participant's attention towards articulating perceptions of coding structures within their environment. Neighbourhood items with which a participant would already be familiar were reproduced on two sheets, each of the items having a problem associated with it which formed a connection between the way it was coded and its function. There were 13 of these kinds of problems leading on to the final subsection which was designed to induce a participant to make imaginative connections between items in his neighbourhood, which were not obviously related. Speculation about the possible was to be an essential part of the project, and this last stage of the first section of the manual introduced a participant to this activity. Reproduced on two sheets called Association Sheet No. 1, and Association Sheet No. 2, were other items from the project areas, each one identified by a letter. These problems directed a participant from Association Sheet No. 1 to No. 2, finally giving him a completely free choice, by asking him to link any of the items on the sheets.

In the second section there were 14 problems, each with a particular area of attention. These were structured into a sequence that started with the inside of a participant's home, and moved to his garden, his street, and finally terminated with ideal states of existence. Thus the problems in this section of the manual were seen as moving from the intimate particular to the ideal general. It was intended that a participant was supposed to answer two problems a day for one week from this sequence. The problems were therefore presented on what were called Day Sheets. The idea behind these was that a more considered response could be obtained from a participant if he answered them over a period of time, rather than if they were all answered together. It was thought unlikely that a person would have the time to answer all the problems at once, and that by structuring the latter section over a period of time, they would be encouraged to complete them in stages. Another factor was that a time lapse between making answers would provide an opportunity for people to reflect on the problems and their answers, before they tackled the next day's problems.

Every page in the manual on which a participant recorded his answers was printed in duplicate; there were 13 of these double pages. A sheet of carbon paper was provided with the manual so that there would be a copy of every entry made by a participant. The top page on which the original was made was loose so that it could be taken out of the manual. On average it took participants about two hours to complete most of the problems in the manual. Not all participants answered all the questions; it is interesting to note that they accepted the linear layout of problems, even though they were told they could start the second section before the first part of the manual if they wanted to. The wider variety of means of expression in the second section of the manual shows that the open nature of the problems was useful in creating a rich response, which can be compared with the first introductory section (see figure 12).

After participants had kept their copy of the West London Manual for three weeks the process of collecting the loose top pages with the original entries began for eventual display. In a large number of cases, when project operators called back for the returns, they found that participants had either only partially completed the manual, or had failed to do so altogether. The reasons for this were:

1 having started a copy of the manual, participants had

found something in it which displeased them, so they had decided to terminate their involvement in the project;
2 participants had just forgotten or, through lack of time, had only partially completed the problems;
3 participants had come to a problem they did not understand.

A special mention should be made here of project area four, Harrow, where not a single return was obtained despite repeated attempts. In the cases of project areas one, two and three, the call for returns prompted participants who had not already done so to finish them. It seems that, having received the manual, participants needed some form of further interaction with the project operators to reassure themselves that their participation was worthwhile. A particularly important feature of the project was that its methods only involved discreet, private interactions, rather than public ones. If a participant had not completed the manual no pressure was put on him to do so, though he was asked if he would like to continue, and if he agreed it was arranged that project operators would call back in ten days' time. Invariably when project operators called back a second time the manuals were completed, though a third attempt was necessary in a few cases. Project area four was the exception, where it seems that for undetermined reasons the project methods were not appropriate. It is interesting that no one in area four seemed to object to the project as such, and a number of people went as far as putting up their window posters.[23] A total of 47 participants completed the manual.

Project operators were becoming familiar with participants at this stage of the project, as they had called on some of them three or four times. As a general principle, as familiarity increased a logical sequence seemed to follow which led the project operators from having the initial introductory conversation on the front door-step, to the next meeting in the hallway, and then finally, after a number of visits, they were asked into the living room. This of course meant that it took project operators longer to get around to seeing all the participants in a project area each time they needed to, though of course it became more interesting to them. During these meetings participants liked to elaborate on their entries in the manual, and to talk about themselves or their neighbourhood. It seems a pity that there was not some way in which these conversations could be fed directly into the project, for in some cases they were more revealing than the person's entries in the manual.

At this stage of the project participants began to draw into it their friends and acquaintances, and more people became interested when the returns from the manual were displayed. Displayed returns represented the first movement in the project's methods from a private context to a more public situation. Returns were to be displayed in public within or near to the project areas on public register boards no. 1 (see figure 13), so that participants could assess their own responses by comparing them with other people's. In looking for suitable sites to house the public register boards, it was important to find a situation with which people from a project area would be familiar in order to minimise the inhibition they might have felt about going there. Such a familiar situation would be a local social resource, and luckily next to each project area was the ideal place in the form of a branch library. There was no trouble in obtaining permission to use the libraries to house the manual's returns and as a result public register boards no. 1 were put up in each area for three weeks. As the illustration shows, the public register boards no. 1 were divided horizontally into three project areas, and vertically into the manual's page numbers, so that a participant could not only easily make comparisons between responses from his own project area, but between other responses as well.

Participants were notified in a circular when public register board no. 1 was going to be displayed and were asked to bring along their carbon copy of the manual to use as the basis for their comparisons. There was no way of checking, but it seems from what participants told project operators that nearly all of them visited the public register boards no. 1, and that the boards' presence in the libraries was starting to create a large neighbourhood secondary audience. The secondary audience was made up of people who had not originally taken part in the project but had either heard about the public registers from participants or had encountered them on their visits to the library. Placing the public aspects of the project within social settings was beginning to succeed, in terms of the numbers of persons becoming involved. Other locations could have been used, such as station entrances, or local shop windows, and they would possibly have been just as successful. From observations made of people studying a public register board, it was ascertained that even casual passers-by spent some ten minutes or so absorbed in what was displayed, and that participants, or their friends, spent on average 20 minutes. While often there were ten to 15 people examining the returns on the public register, they did not appear to communicate with each other. Though people were publicly interacting with each other, they were doing so in a more discreet way through the project's methods or by personal contact with other participants. The display of returns from the manual represented the middle point of the project, though it took longer to reach than anticipated.

In order to speed up the next stage of the project we decided to reorganise the project operators into three teams, each of which would be responsible for its own project area for the duration of the project. Though the original motive in forming teams was for reasons of economy, it also had another function which perhaps ultimately was more important, and this involved the relationship of the project operators to participants. With one mobile team of project operators there was a high chance that each time a participant answered his door to a project operator he would be faced with an unfamiliar person, while on the other hand a small permanent team would become increasingly familiar, and thus help to create a more mutual relationship between the two. It was anticipated that this would increase project operator identification with a project area, which we thought would be important in maintaining their involvement in the second stage of the project.

Project operators were given the choice of which team they wanted to join, and most did so in accordance with the participant group they personally felt some affinity to. The next stage of the project involved participants in a process of re-modelling the descriptive models they had made in the first stage into prescriptive ones. The initial agent in the re-modelling process was a companion booklet to the manual, similar in design, called the West London Re-modelling Book (see figure 14). While the problems in the re-modelling book pointed to similar areas of attention as those of the manual, their orientation was quite different. Problems enabled a participant to make speculative reorderings from their descriptive models, which were formed around what they ideally expected from their immediate environment (see figure 15). The problems in the re-modelling book were structured as a sequence that started from an intimate context (a participant's own home) and progressed by degrees to a more general conceptual situation (a participant's neighbourhood community's ideal social structure). The number of problems was kept to a minimum as it was recognised that they required more thought and time from a participant, than those presented in the manual. Problems led into each other, the intention being that completed ones should be used as a basis for future solutions. For example, the community garden problem (see figure 15) directed a participant's attention towards the physical layout of his environment, and its effect on social relationships. The next problem continued in this direction, but centred on the role of social resources within the community. These problems finally led to participants being asked what they saw as the ideal social structure of their neighbourhood, and its relationship to other communities in west London.

When project operators went to their respective project areas to give participants the re-modelling book, they found that two or three wished to terminate their involvement with the project. The participant numbers were made up by the people who wanted to join in for the second stage of the project, and were further enlarged by some of the original participants actively involving their family, neighbours, friends, etc., in compiling solutions to the problems. In some cases a person jointly participated with someone else all through the project; in other instances a number of participants' friends all sat down together to formulate solutions as a group activity, rather in the way they might have played cards or watched television. Entries in the re-modelling book showed the same variety of expression as in the manual, though participants found it much harder to complete. Problems that participants found difficult were the ones about how they would organise cultural activities, and especially the final one which concerned their ideal neighbourhood social structure. In a few cases participants only completed the descriptive section of the two-part problems at the front, leaving blank the more conceptual re-modelling stage.

the last stage of the project

Participants were given three weeks to complete the re-modelling book, before their team of project operators called to collect the top copies of entries. On this occasion too, though less than in the first stage, some of the participants had not completed all of the problems. However, after a second call they were nearly all fully completed. One effect of allocating a team to look after a particular project area was that the response from participants reflected the enthusiasm or commitment of the project operator. Returns from the re-modelling book were all gathered together, and then displayed on public register boards no. 2 (see figure 16). Sheets from the re-modelling book were displayed on the board according to their page number in columns. Each sheet within a particular column was given a letter, so that it was possible to identify an individual return, and so that participants could record their preferences from the models on display. This was the central part of the final stage of the project, which was intended to generate a series of consensus models, termed final project models. These represented a culmination of a participant's involvement with the project.

A participant could then compare the consensus against his own entries in his re-modelling book and in his manual. The consensus view was ascertained by means of votes. Preferences were recorded on public decision slips (figure 17). More than the simple cross normally associated with voting procedures was required from a person completing one of the public decision slips, for they were also given the opportunity to comment on the reason for their choice, or to propose alterations to the displayed models.

Voting was not restricted to participants: anyone who was interested in the content of the displayed returns could fill in one of the slips. The siting of the boards in branch libraries adjacent to the project areas tended to limit the people who filled in slips to residents from the neighbourhood. The identity of people who filled in the slips was not recorded, so the percentage of participants who did vote cannot be calculated accurately; but from casual observations and information offered spontaneously an estimate can be made of approximately 60 per cent. Most completed decision slips also included added comments or observations about the choices that had been made. In making a selection from the displayed returns, people invariably chose some that were from project areas other than their own, and as a result they were fulfilling the intended conjoining process which was the last stage of the project.

The boards stayed at each library for a period of three weeks, during which time residents in the project areas were sent leaflets telling them when the boards would visit their neighbourhood and explaining the voting system. The consensus tendencies were constructed from a straight count of all the preferences shown on the public decision slips, regardless of the project area they originated from. The full list of votes cast is shown in figure 18. The returns with the most votes were those that formed the final project models, and these were reproduced in a booklet with the same title (see figure 19). In a number of cases there was an equal number of votes for two returns from the same page in the re-modelling book: in these cases both were reproduced. It is difficult for an outsider to assess the significance of the content of individual returns making up the final project models, as the references are all dependent on the daily lives of residents within the project areas. The final project model booklet was delivered to all participants, and copies were also left at the local library for the secondary audience to pick up. Participants who had retained copies of both their manual and their re-modelling book as a documentation of their involvement in the project could then add the final project models. They could make their own comparisons and draw their own conclusions. The delivery of the final project models to participants was the last stage of the project; after this no attempt was made to find out the project's long-term effects.[24]

evaluation of the project's performance

In attempting an evaluation of the project, it is important to bear in mind the largely experimental nature of its methods when looking at the relationship between its theoretical intentions and what was achieved in practice. Ideologically I saw the project as a demonstration that an artwork would meaningfully operate outside art's social environment, as an integral part of people's social reality. The project was largely successful in achieving this objective, in that starting from a situation where it was not known what response, if any, would be obtained, two thirds of the people who agreed to participate did so for its duration. It is reasonable to assume that people would not have sustained their involvement in the project unless they found its concerns, or the act of participating, relevant to themselves in some way.

The unexpected generation of a large and interested secondary audience is a further indication that the project was more generally relevant to people in the neighbourhoods in which it took place than just to participants. As a large secondary audience was unexpected, they were not considered in the planning stage of the project as a positive element in successful communicative performance. However, when it became clear during the operation of the project that a secondary audience was emerging, the project was sufficiently flexible to involve them at the level they had chosen. Anyone could express a preference for different participant models by voting during the project's final stages. (In subsequent works, such as the one discussed in the next chapter, the creation of a secondary audience was seen from the outset as integral to the communicative function of the works.)

While generally the project can be considered to have achieved one of its intentions, in demonstrating the externalisation of art, it certainly cannot be considered to have worked in the case of project area four, Harrow, the upper middle-class social group. As previously mentioned, there is no conclusive evidence as to why the project did not work in this area. People seemed enthusiastic enough at the start, though as interest dropped when they were given the West London Manual to complete – their first task – it is reasonable to assume that to have been the cause. What might have seemed acceptable as a concept during the introductory stages of the project was much less so when participants were asked to carry it through in practice. Perhaps the project as an operating entity undermined certain values, such as territorial privacy, that this social group might have felt strongly about, though this is all conjecture and in other projects, such as the one discussed in the next chapter, similar social groups were involved, and they participated as fully as any other.

While the creation of the project was intended to demonstrate the externalisation of art, its specified objectives as a work of art derived from considering problems of social function. As a result the project's objectives were directly concerned with changing participants' perceptions of coding structures within their neighbourhood environment, rather than how they perceived the activity 'art'. While no systematic investigation was made into the effect of the project on participants, they did carry out the intended re-modelling procedures. If the procedures of the project were carried out by a participant, then there is little doubt that they would have effected a change in their own cognition. This is because of the nature of the tasks participants were given, each one requiring a possible shift in the way a person perceived what was, or had become through habit, a set coded feature of their environment. The act of recording in a communicable form a response to a problem, meant a participant ordering explicitly what were implicit shifts in perception. The accumulative linear nature of problems meant that changes in perception gradually built up, varying as they did so from previously established norms. This is of course what was intended, and in this respect it is interesting to compare the returns from the manual with those of the re-modelling book. While the manual asked for a more descriptive response, it still required shifts in the way participants perceived their surroundings, and these can be seen in the way the participants coded their returns. People were for the first time looking at their environment's coding structures within a formal perceptual framework. With the re-modelling book a more prescriptive shift in perception was required in forming a response, and in a number of cases participants were unable to make the necessary rearticulations.

In the operation of the West London Project, the gap between major events, such as a participant receiving his copy of the manual at the beginning of the project and the voting at the end, was undoubtedly too long. It would have been too much to expect participants to have retained their completed copies of the manual for the three months or so before the end of the project, without the active part they played in viewing public register boards no. 1. In retrospect it was unfortunate that the project extended for as long as it did. It would have been more compact over the six-month period originally intended. Without doubt the success of the public register boards held the project together. The public exposure of what were underlying neighbourhood relationships stimulated people's curiosity, and created new perceptions between them. At the end of the project participants often voted for returns from project areas other than their own, indicating that those returns were studied and compared with their own neighbourhoods. This in itself must have affected participants' models of social groups other than their own.

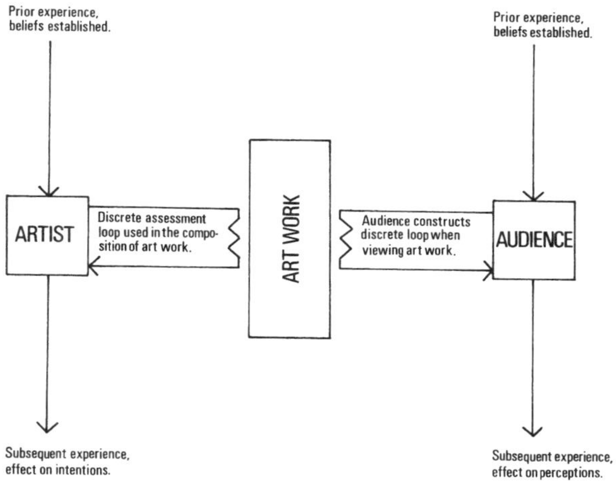

FIGURE 1 Diagram shows the position an artwork traditionally occupies between the artist and his audience. Two fundamental discrete cognate loops are shown, which are isolated from each other by the artwork. There is no form of interaction beteen the two which could generate mutual understanding as would be the case in a successful conversation. In the absence of such a procedure both the audience and the artist become locked in their own perceptual biases.

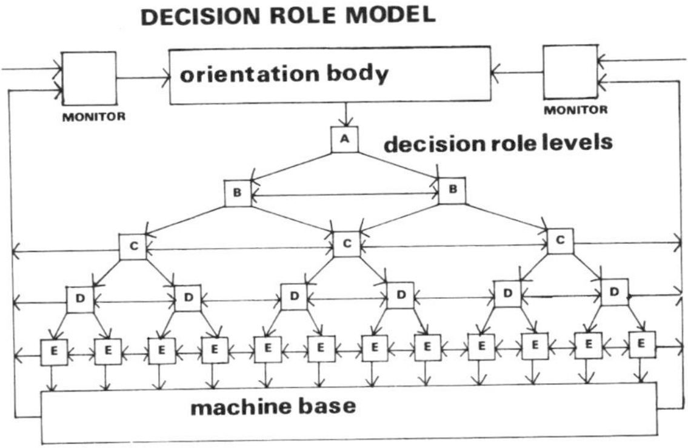

FIGURE 2 An abstraction of the decision-making procedures that are typical of those employed in present-day social organisations within western culture. The decision tree filters information from the orientation body to the machine base.

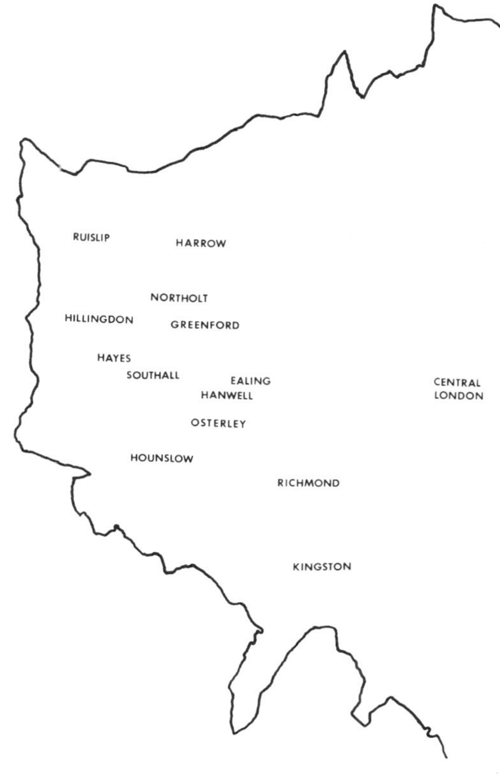

FIGURE 3 The area of west London considered for the project.

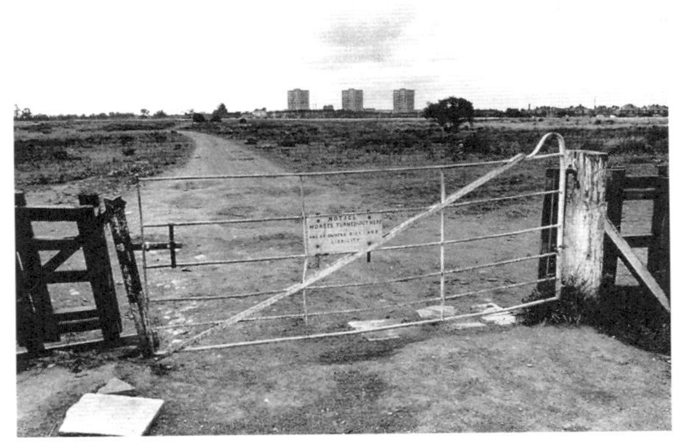

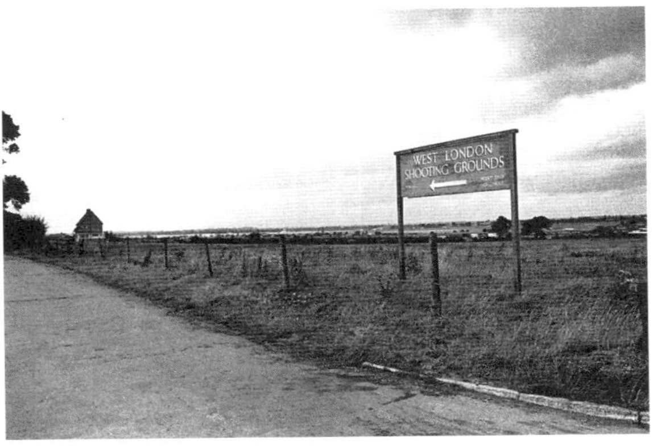

FIGURE 4 Examples from the series of reconnaissance pictures of the West London Waste Lands taken by Mick Marshal.

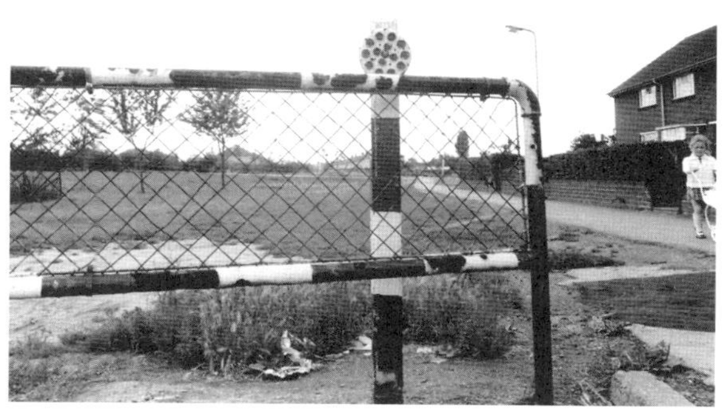

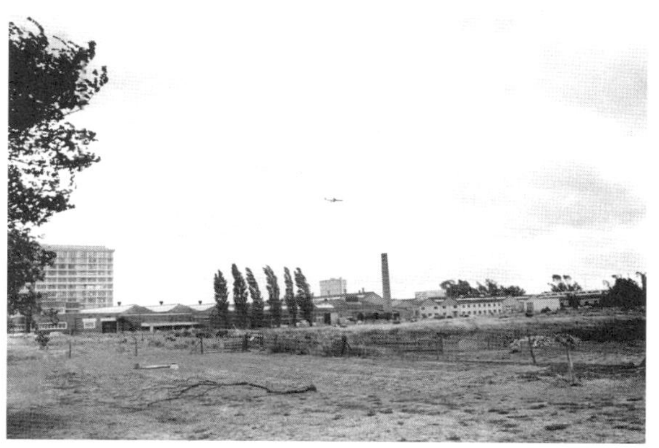

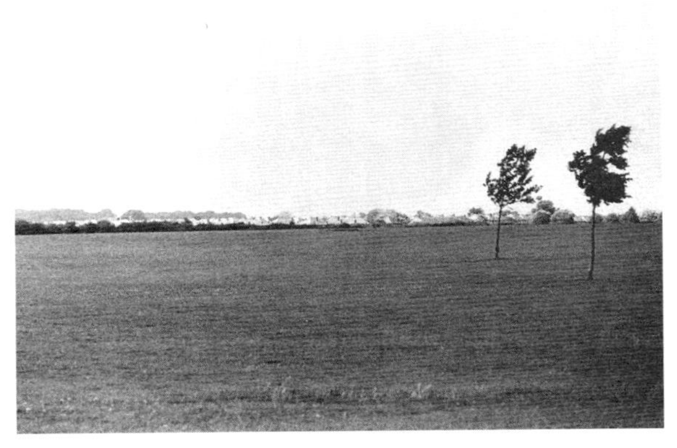

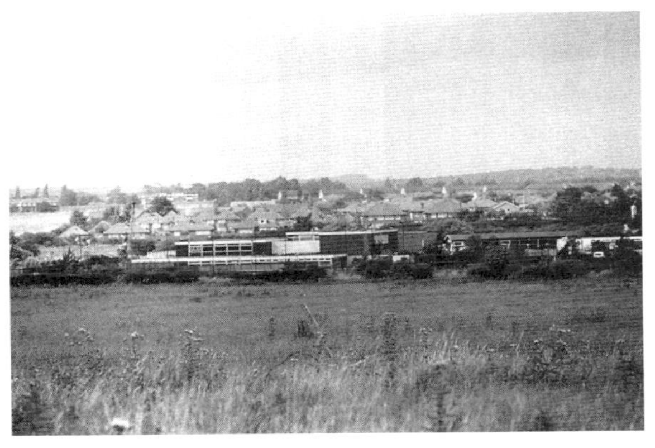

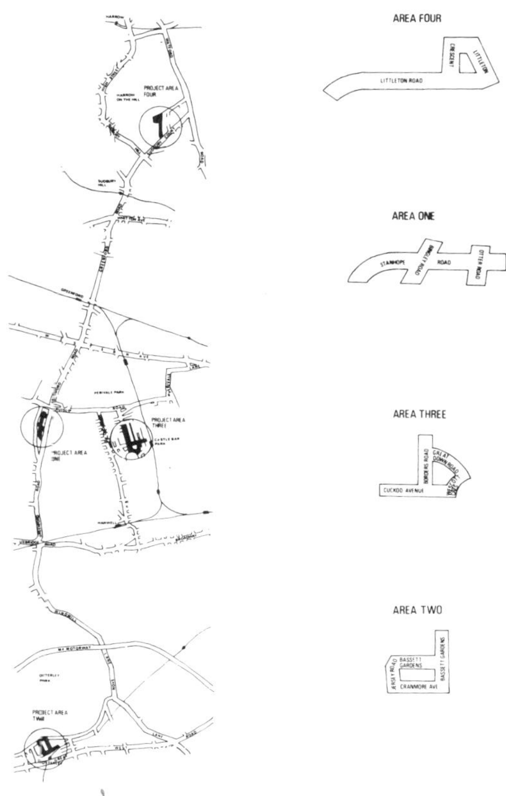

FIGURE 5 Relationship of project areas to each other in west London.

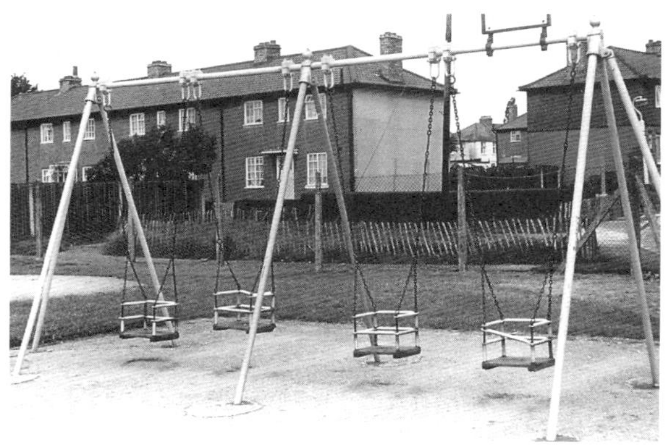

Project area one: Greenford

Project area three: Hanwell

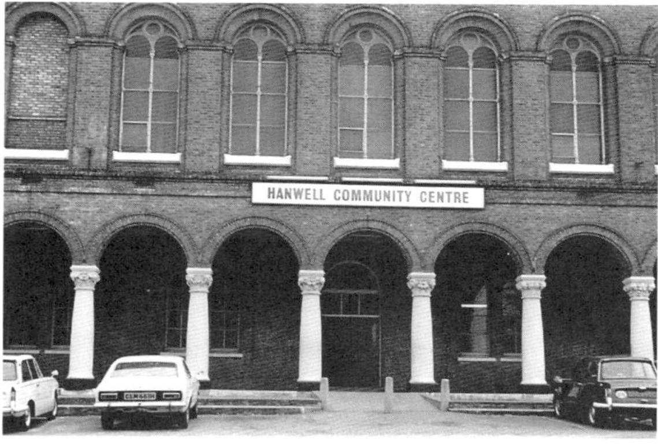

FIGURE 6A Examples of what were considered local resources by residents of project areas.

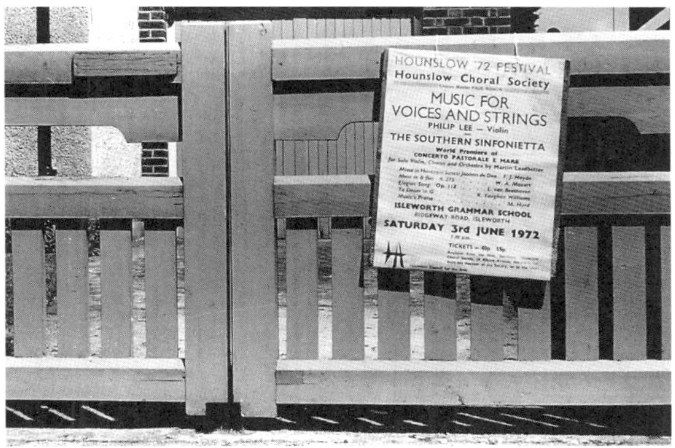

Project area two: Osterley

Project area four: Harrow

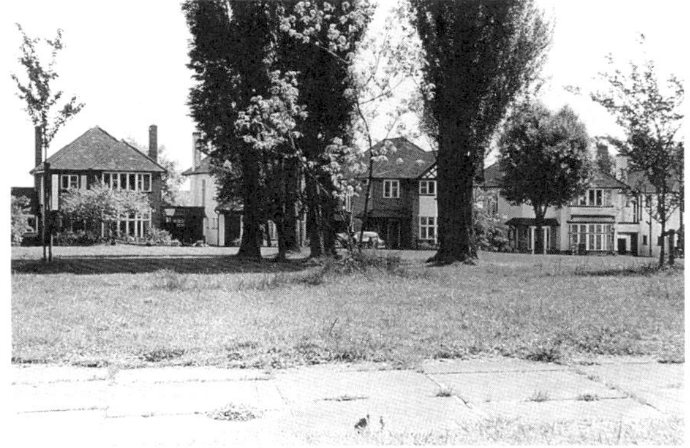

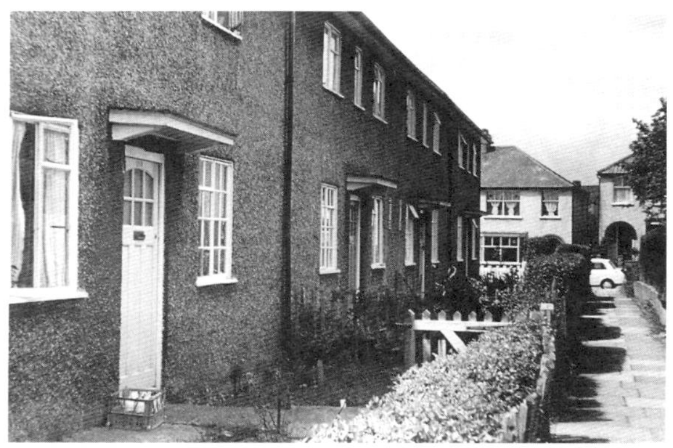

Project area one: Greenford

Project area three: Hanwell

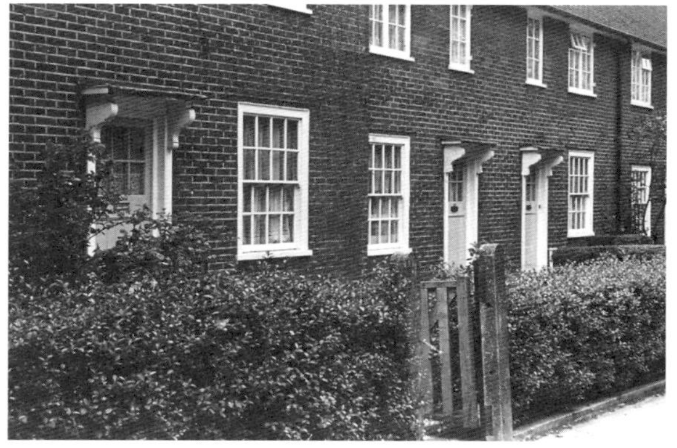

FIGURE 6B Participant houses that were typical of each project area.

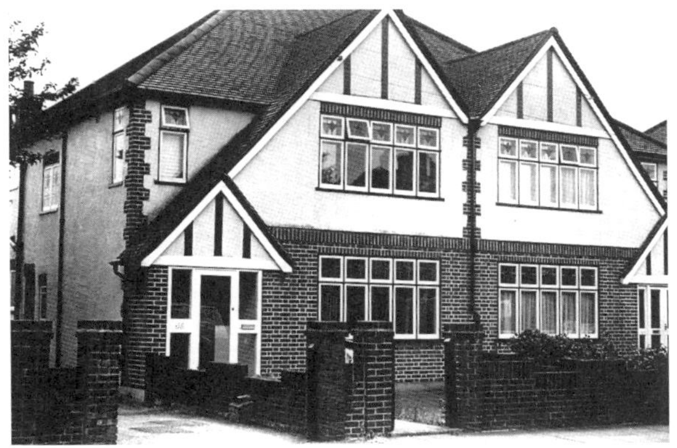

Project area two: Osterley

Project area four: Harrow

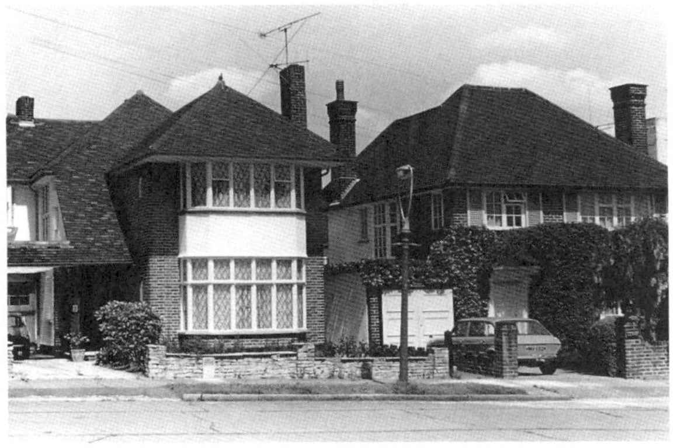

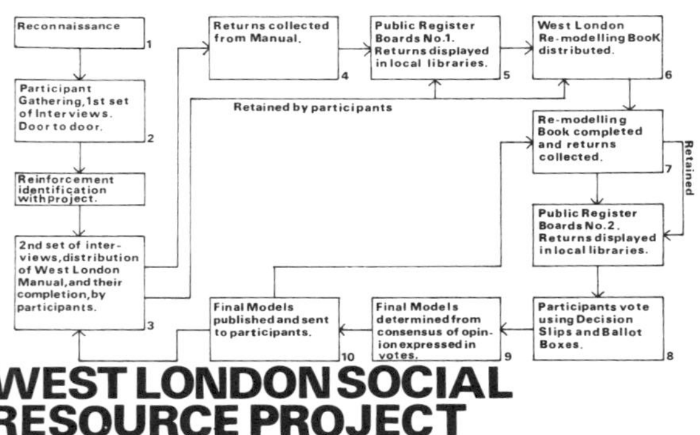

FIGURE 7 Flow diagram of the project as a linear structure through time.

During July a project is being run called the West London Social Resource Project, which is about West London, and is aimed at the people that live there. The project sets up environmental conditions that enable participants in the project to perceive their social/physical environment in ways that can't be viewed when entrenched within existing routines. The results of this are recorded and a synthesis made that establishes a criteria for the participants to remodel aspects of their social environment in ways that they feel they control and determine.

Four social groups that come from West London, but see each other as physically, economically, socially separate, form the basis of the project, and it's from these groups that participants are invited. The project is structured so that interaction between participants forms the basis of a language which enables meaningful communication and insight to be achieved between the groups involved. The project also seeks to demonstrate that the artist can meaningfully communicate to people outside the art environment, and is somewhat in the nature of an experiment, using as it will strategies that owe nothing to those used within the art environment.

A group of people are being gathered from a variety of backgrounds to enable the structure of the project, part of which are the West London Super Girls.

Six girls called the West London Super Girls are required to help participate in designing and operating the project, this leaflet is an invitation to join this group. It is important that none of the six girls know of the others so that the only history they have in common is that of the project. This is to ensure a natural grouping on the project which is not biased by previous associations, hence this leaflet being handed to you in the street.

FIGURE 8 Extracts from the West London Super Girl leaflet.

WEST LONDON SOCIAL RESOURCE PROJECT

The West London Social Resource Project attempts to determine what social /physical environment you and the community in the area you live in see as serving your actual needs.

Initially it asks you to examine your exsisting environment in order to ascertain what perceptions, attitudes, behaviours exsist, and at what level does it relate to your needs. The project also shows you how other people in three different areas in West London feel about their environment, and their proposals for one built around what they consider their needs to be.

Thus it helps you obtain insight, understanding in to the environment you live in, showing how you relate to it, and how it relates to others.

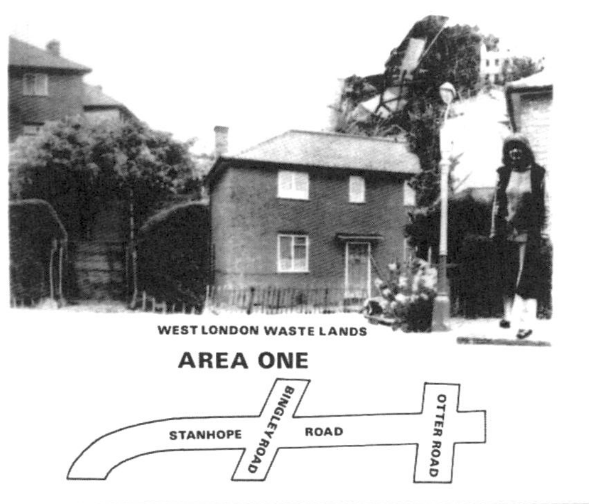

FIGURE 9 Project area information leaflets.

WEST LONDON SOCIAL RESOURCE PROJECT

The West London Social Resource Project attempts to determine what social/physical environment you and the community in the area you live in see as serving your actual needs.
Initially it asks you to examine your exsisting environment in order to ascertain what perceptions, attitudes, behaviours exsist, and at what level does it relate to your needs.
The project also shows you how other people in three different areas in West London feel about their environment, and their proposals for one built around what they consider their needs to be.
Thus it helps you obtain insight, understanding in to the environment you live in, showing how you relate to it, and how it relates to others.

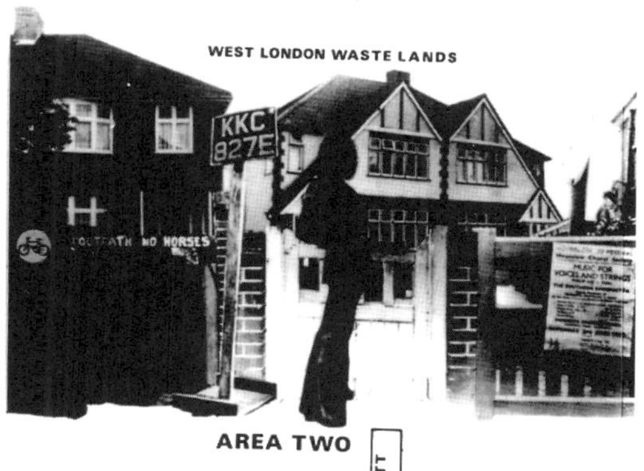

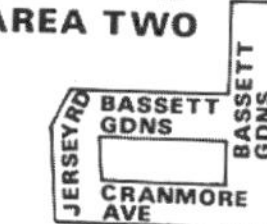

WEST LONDON SOCIAL RESOURCE PROJECT

The West London Social Resource Project attempts to determine what social/physical environment you and the community in the area you live in see as serving your actual needs.
Initially it asks you to examine you exsisting environment in order to ascertain what perceptions, attitudes, behaviours exsist, and at what level does it relate to your needs.
The project also shows you how other people in three different areas in West London feel about their environment, and their proposals for one built around what they consider their needs to be.
Thus it helps you obtain insight, understanding of the environment you live in, showing how you relate to it, and how it relates to others.

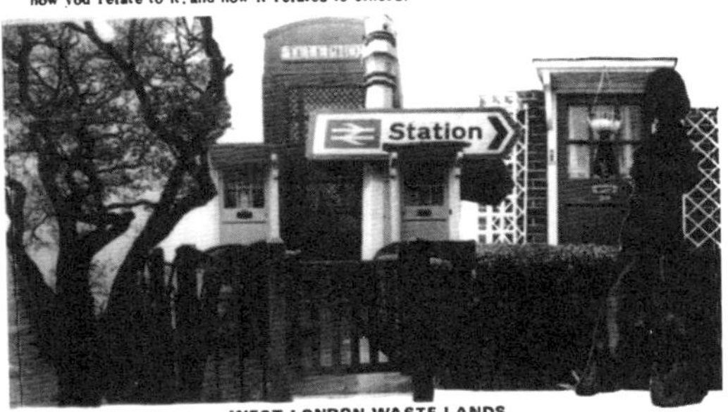

WEST LONDON WASTE LANDS

AREA THREE

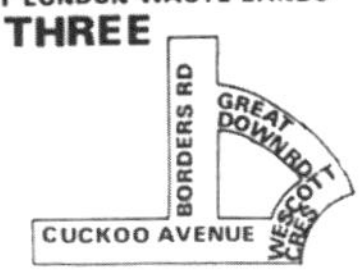

WEST LONDON SOCIAL RESOURCE PROJECT

The West London Social Resource Project attempts to determine what social/physical environment you and the community in the area you live in see as serving your actual needs.
Initially it asks you to examine your exsisting environment in order to ascertain what perceptions, attitudes, behaviours exsist, and at what level does it relate to your needs.
The project also shows you how other people in three different areas in West London feel about their environment, and their proposals for one built around what they consider their needs to be.
Thus it helps you obtain insight, understanding of your environment, showing how you relate to it, and how it relates to others.

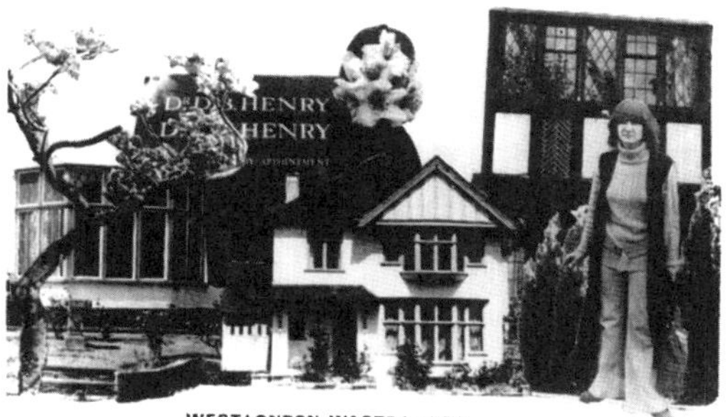

WESTLONDON WASTE LANDS

AREA FOUR

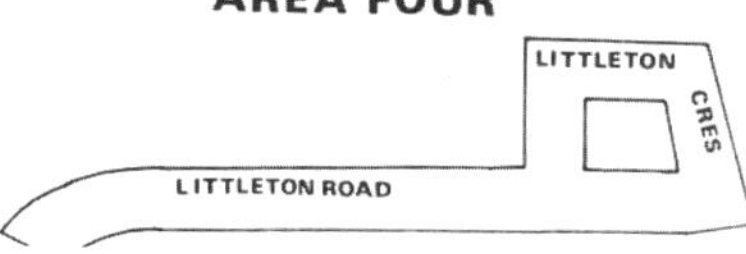

WEST LONDON SOCIAL RESOURCE PROJECT

PARTICIPANT NO ....

PHOTO
OF
PARTICPANT

AREA ONE

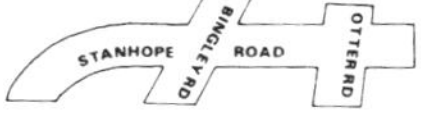

FIGURE 10 Two of the project area window posters that were to be displayed by participants at the front of their houses.

WEST LONDON SOCIAL RESOURCE PROJECT

PARTICIPANT NO ....

PHOTO
OF
PARTICPANT

AREA TWO

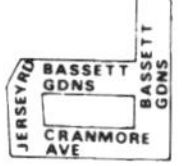

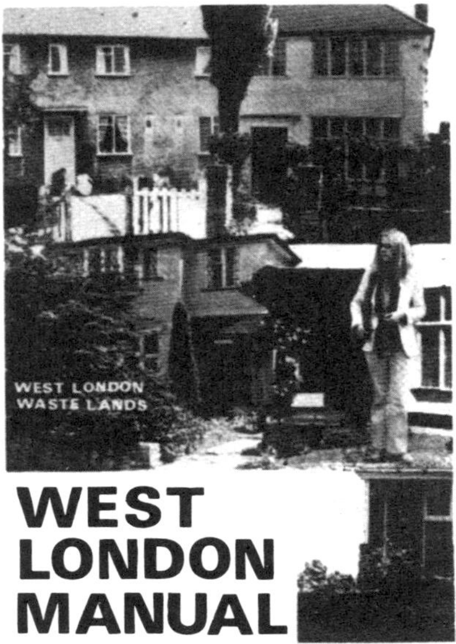

FIGURE 11 The front cover and other pages from the West London Manual that contained subject matter for the problems.

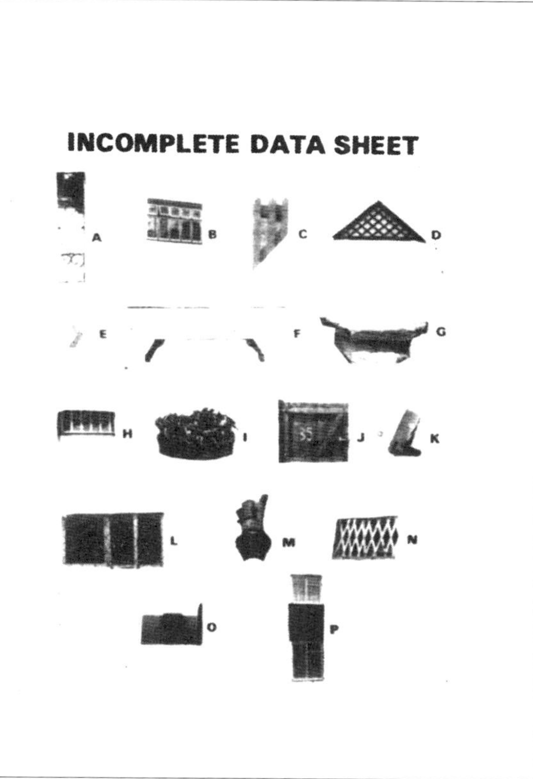
INCOMPLETE DATA SHEET
A
B
C
D
E
F
G
H
I
J
K
L
M
N
O
P

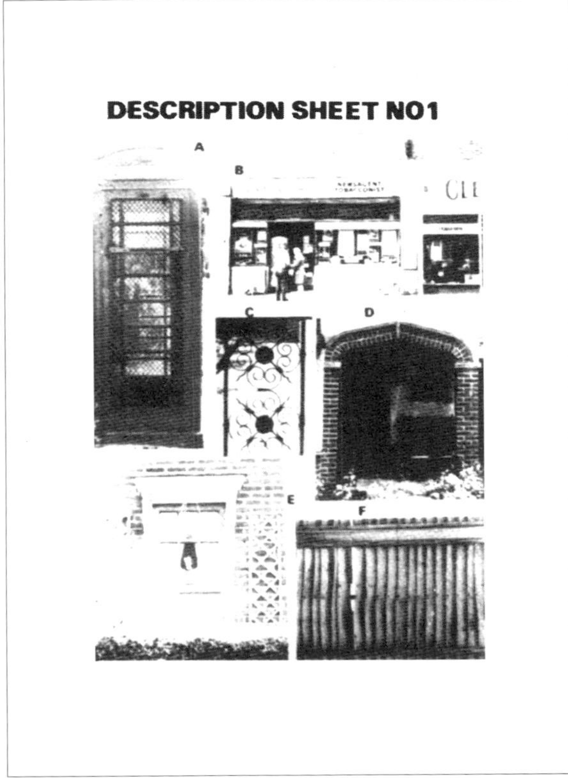
DESCRIPTION SHEET NO1
A
B
C
D
E
F

DESCRIPTION SHEET NO 2

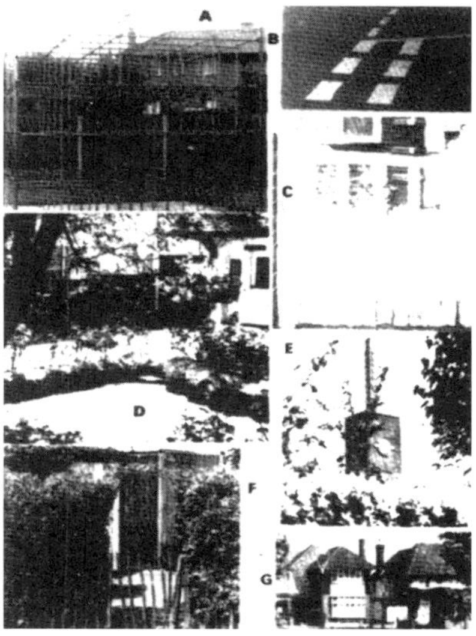

COMPLETE DATA SHEET NO1

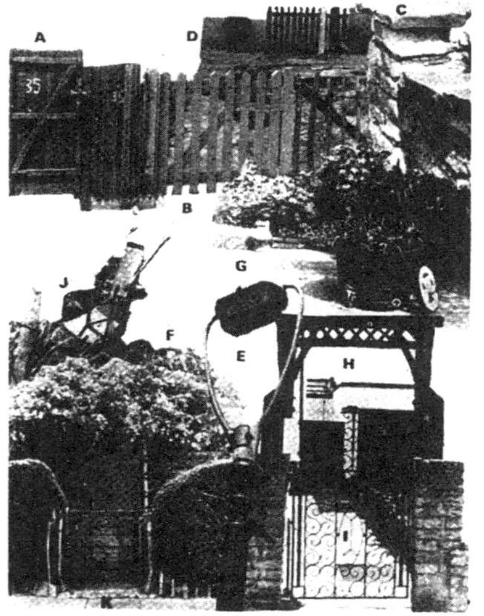

COMPLETE DATA SHEET NO2

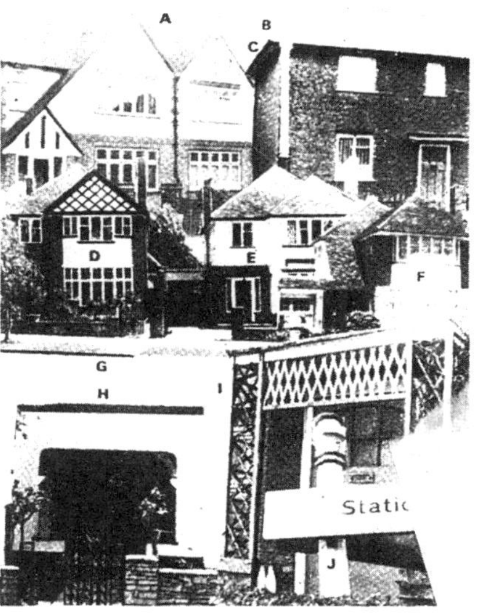

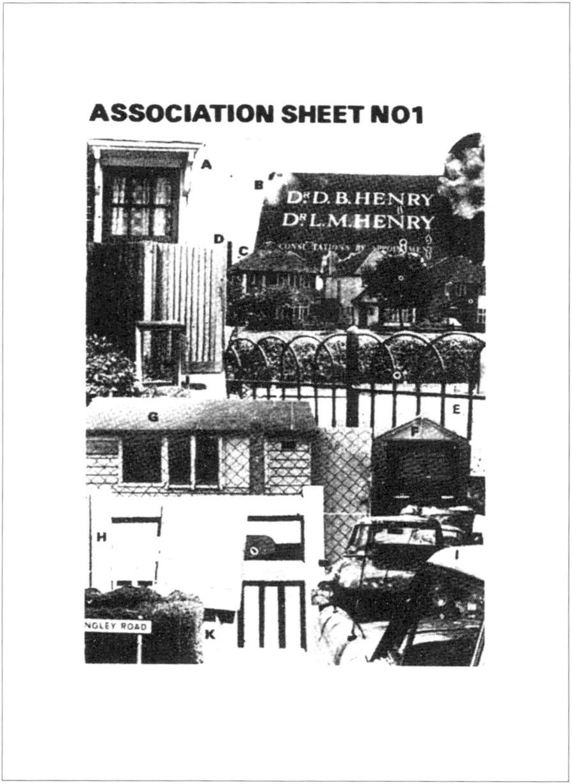

ASSOCIATION SHEET NO1

ASSOCIATION SHEET NO 2

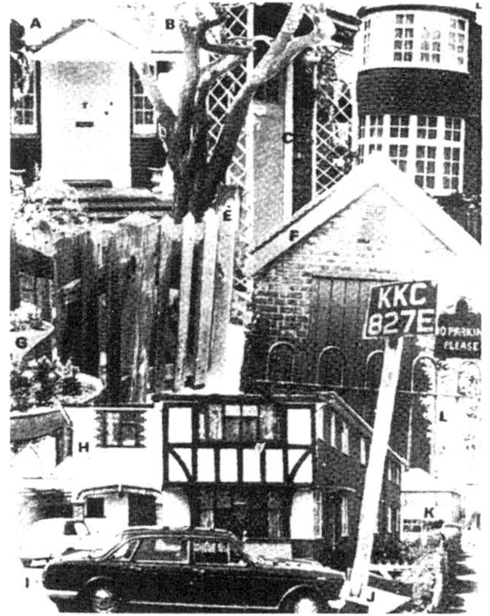

FIGURE 12 West London Manual

The following pages show examples of participant returns from the West London Manual. The returns illustrated here were selected solely because they were suitable for the reproducing process, and have not been singled out for any reasons of merit associated with content. Sheets from the first part of the manual should be studied in connection with those in figure 11.

ON THE INCOMPLETE DATA SHEET AT THE BACK OF THE MANUAL ARE A SERIES OF INCOMPLETE OBJECTS/PHOTOGRAPHS LETTERED A-P: CAN YOU IDENTIFY THE COMPLETE OBJECT/PHOTOGRAPH FROM THE COMPLETE DATA SHEETS RECORDING THE SHEET NUMBER AND LETTER. THEN CAN YOU DESCRIBE ASSOCIATIONS THAT YOU HAVE WITH THE COMPLETE OBJECT/PHOTOGRAPH.

INCOMPLETE OBJECT A
COMPLETE OBJECT SHEET NO. 1 ... OBJECT LETTER. I ...
DESCRIBE YOUR ASSOCIATIONS. I REALISED BY THE SHAPE OF OBJECT A, THAT IT WAS AN ORNATE GATE, SO SET ABOUT LOOKING FOR ONE ON COMPLETE DATA SHEE I

INCOMPLETE OBJECT B
COMPLETE OBJECT SHEET NO. 2 ... OBJECT LETTER. A ...
DESCRIBE YOUR ASSOCIATIONS. OBVIOUSLY A WINDOW – JUST A QUESTION OF FINDING THE CORRECT ONE.

INCOMPLETE OBJECT C
COMPLETE OBJECT SHEET NO. 1 ... OBJECT LETTER. B ...
DESCRIBE YOUR ASSOCIATIONS. AS IN OBJECT B, EXCEPT THIS TIME IT IS A GATE.

INCOMPLETE OBJECT D
COMPLETE OBJECT SHEET NO. 2 ... OBJECT LETTER. D ...
DESCRIBE YOUR ASSOCIATIONS. NOTICED THE SHARP CONTRAST IN LATTICE WORK AND ITS BACKGROUND.

INCOMPLETE OBJECT E
COMPLETE OBJECT SHEET NO. 7 ... OBJECT LETTER. J ...
DESCRIBE YOUR ASSOCIATIONS. SAW IT WAS ARROW-HEAD; ONLY ONE DIRECTION-INDICATOR IN PHOTOS

INCOMPLETE OBJECT F
COMPLETE OBJECT SHEET NO. 2 ... OBJECT LETTER. H ...
DESCRIBE YOUR ASSOCIATIONS. SAME AS INCOMPLETE OBJECT B

INCOMPLETE OBJECT N
COMPLETE OBJECT SHEET NO...2.OBJECT LETTER..I..
DESCRIBE YOUR ASSOCIATIONS.............................
.UNEVOCATIVE...TRELLISWORK.............................
....

INCOMPLETE OBJECT O
COMPLETE OBJECT SHEET NO...1..OBJECT LETTER.D...
DESCRIBE YOUR ASSOCIATIONS..ANY....BACKGARDEN
.OR...EQUIVALENT..
....

INCOMPLETE OBJECT P
COMPLETE OBJECT SHEET NO..2.OBJECT LETTER.C...
DESCRIBE YOUR ASSOCIATIONS..ANY....COUNCIL......
.HOUSE...
....

DISPLAYED ON THE DESCRIPTION SHEETS NO 1 AND NO 2 AT THE BACK OF THE MANUAL ARE A SERIES OF PHOTOGRAPHS TAKEN FROM THE FOUR AREAS TAKING PART IN THE PROJECT. YOU ARE NOW ASKED TO MAKE DESCRIPTIONS ABOUT THEM.

DESCRIPTION SHEET NO 1

DESCRIBE THE USES OF A BY YOU AND THE PEOPLE IN YOUR STREET....OCCASIONAL....COMMUNICATION
.WITH..NOT..QUITE..'LOCAL'..ACQUAINTANCES...
.WHO..HAVE..A PRIVATE..PHONE..........................
CAN YOU DESCRIBE A TYPICAL B IN YOUR NEIGHBOURHOOD
.TYPICAL..'B's'...IN...THE...NEIGHBOURHOOD...
..ARE...SIMILAR..TO..THAT...ONE..SHOWN..IN.
THE..PHOTOGRAPH..EXCEPT,PERHAPS,..THAT.....
THERE..IS..LESS..ADVERTISING..IN..THE..WINDOWS..AND...
MORE..OF..THE..ACTUAL..PRODUCT.........................
HOW DOES THIS FEATURE ON A GATE RELATE TO THE SOCIAL STANDING OF THE OCCUPANTS OF THE HOUSE IT STANDS IN FRONT OF IN C...IT..REPRESENTS..AT.....
.LEAST..ONE..STEP..UP..A..HYPOTHETICAL.......
.SOCIAL..LADDER...

DESCRIBE [illegible] TO YOUR NEIGHBOURHOOD COMMUNITY. THE RIGHT NOT TO HAVE TO MAKE THE PLACE LOOK PRESENTABLE

WHAT KIND OF LIFE STYLE DO YOU ATTACH TO THE OWNERS OF THE HOUSES IN G. ROUTINE, MORE AFFLUENT THAN AVERAGE, THOUGH, SOME KIND OF EXECUTIVE AS THE HEAD OF FAMILY IS POSSIBLE.

AT THE BACK OF THE MANUAL ARE TWO ASSOCIATION SHEETS. LINK ONE OF THE OBJECTS/PHOTOGRAPHS ON SHEET 1 WITH ONE ON SHEET 2 AND DESCRIBE WHAT ASSOCIATIONS YOU ARE ABLE TO MAKE.

ASSOCIATION SHEET 1

OBJECT A LINKED WITH SHEET 2 OBJECT LETTER. S
NOW DESCRIBE YOUR ASSOCIATIONS.
FRONT VIEW OF COUNCIL HOUSE

OBJECT B LINKED WITH SHEET 2 OBJECT LETTER. P
DESCRIBE YOUR ASSOCIATIONS.
SEMI DETACHED, WAITING ROOM WELL KEPT HOUSE, CLEAR ATMOSPHERE

OBJECT C LINKED WITH SHEET 2 OBJECT LETTER. Q
DESCRIBE YOUR ASSOCIATIONS.
HOUSE WELL DIMINISHED BY SURROUNDING GREENERY

OBJECT D LINKED WITH SHEET 2 OBJECT LETTER. E
DESCRIBE YOUR ASSOCIATIONS.
USUAL QUICKLY PRODUCED GATES AND FENCING

DESCRIBE WHAT F MEANS TO YOUR NEIGHBOURHOOD COMMUNITY ?

WHAT KIND OF LIFE STYLE DO YOU ATTACH TO THE OWNERS OF THE HOUSES IN G... RATHER WEALTHY. HUSBAND + WIFE BOTH WORKING. CHILDREN EDUCATED AT PRIVATE SCHOOL. HUSBAND LIKES ENTERTAINING AT HOME A LOT.

AT THE BACK OF THE MANUAL ARE TWO ASSOCIATION SHEETS. LINK ONE OF THE OBJECTS/PHOTOGRAPHS ON SHEET 1 WITH ONE ON SHEET 2 AND DESCRIBE WHAT ASSOCIATIONS YOU ARE ABLE TO MAKE.

ASSOCIATION SHEET 1

OBJECT A LINKED WITH SHEET 2 OBJECT LETTER G

NOW DESCRIBE YOUR ASSOCIATIONS. ASSOCIATED WITH EACH OTHER AS BOTH OBVIOUSLY COUNCIL HOUSES.

OBJECT B LINKED WITH SHEET 2 OBJECT LETTER F

DESCRIBE YOUR ASSOCIATIONS. NO PARKING OUTSIDE DOCTORS ENTRANCE.

OBJECT C LINKED WITH SHEET 2 OBJECT LETTER

DESCRIBE YOUR ASSOCIATIONS. ?

OBJECT D LINKED WITH SHEET 2 OBJECT LETTER K

DESCRIBE YOUR ASSOCIATIONS. HOUSES LIKE THOSE ON SHEET 2 LETTER K, OFF STANHOPE ROAD (IN ALLEY LEADING TO WINDMILL LANE) HAVE FENCING LIKE OBJECT D.

Project area one: Greenford

WITH PHOTOGRAPH D DESCRIBE WHAT KIND OF PHANTASY PROJECTION YOU ASSOCIATE THIS FEATURE WITH.........

REMINDS ME OF A FIRE-PLACE IN TUDOR TIMES !

DESCRIBE WHAT FUNCTION THE OBJECTS THAT MAKE UP E HAVE.

TRELLIS-WORK IS FOR GROWING CLIMBING PLANTS. OTHER FOR ORDINARY PLANTS.

DESCRIBE WHAT SOCIAL ROLE F HAS.

MAKES GARDEN PRIVATE, KEEPS DOGS, CHILDREN ETC OUT. CAN ISOLATE PEOPLE THOUGH

DESCRIPTION SHEET NO 2

WHAT SOCIAL FUNCTION DOES A HAVE.

AMUSES CHILDREN. ENABLES CHILDREN TO MEET NEW FRIENDS WHEN THEY PLAY IN PARK.

DESCRIBE WHAT B MEANS IN YOUR NEIGHBOURHOOD.

(STOP AND GIVE PRIORITY TO TRAFFIC ALREADY ON EXIT ROAD OR SLOW DOWN IF EXIT ROAD CLEAR)

DESCRIBE WHAT FUNCTION YOU THINK A FRONT GATE HAS

IN THIS AREA TO KEEP OUT CHILDREN AND DOGS. ALSO TO KEEP OUR DOG IN !

WHAT SOCIAL DISPLAY FUNCTION DOES D HAVE.

A STATUS SYMBOL (TO A CERTAIN EXTENT) UNLESS SOMEONE CARES FOR THEIR GARDEN BECAUSE HE ENJOYS GARDENING

DESCRIBE THE ROLE E HAS IN AFFECTING THE SOCIAL BEHAVIOUR OF WEST LONDON.

PEOPLE HAVE EASY ACCESS TO CENTRE OF LONDON VIA UNDERGROUND. TEND TO GO TO WEST END MORE FOR ENTERTAINMENT ETC THAN IF THERE WERE NO UNDERGROUND

WITH PHOTOGRAPH D DESCRIBE WHAT KIND OF PHANTASY PROJECTION YOU ASSOCIATE THIS FEATURE WITH.........

LARGER ROOMS, WELL ESTABLISHED FAMILY PERHAPS CHILDLESS

DESCRIBE WHAT FUNCTION THE OBJECTS THAT MAKE UP E HAVE. THEY HIGHLIGHT WHAT THEY APPEAR TO BE TRYING TO HIDE, ie THE FRONT VIEW OF ANOTHER COUNCIL HOUSE

DESCRIBE WHAT SOCIAL ROLE F HAS.....................

IS HAS NONE, OR IS ANTISOCIAL

DESCRIPTION SHEET NO 2

WHAT SOCIAL FUNCTION DOES A HAVE...................

PROVIDES SOME STIMULATION FOR SOME CHILDREN

DESCRIBE WHAT B MEANS IN YOUR NEIGHBOURHOOD........

THE IMPORTANCE OF THE MOTOR CAR

DESCRIBE WHAT FUNCTION YOU THINK A FRONT GATE HAS

OBSTRUCTS UNWANTED VISITORS, DOGS, ETC, GIVES A SENSE OF OWNERSHIP, STATUS, PRIVACY ETC.

WHAT SOCIAL DISPLAY FUNCTION DOES D HAVE..........

IMPROVES APPEARANCE OF THE PLACE

DESCRIBE THE ROLE E HAS IN AFFECTING THE SOCIAL BEHAVIOUR OF WEST LONDON...........................

NEGLIGIBLE

THE DAY SHEETS ARE MEANT TO BE USED AFTER YOU HAVE FILLED IN THE FIRST PART OF THE BOOK, THERE BEING SEVEN SHEETS, ONE FOR EACH DAY OF THE WEEK, PLEASE FILL THEM IN CONSECUTIVELY. IF THERE IS NOT ENOUGH ROOM ON THE FRONT OF THE PAGE PLEASE USE THE BACK.

SUNDAY SHEET 1
DESCRIBE/DRAW/MAKE A PLAN OF WHAT IS ON YOUR MANTLEPIECE

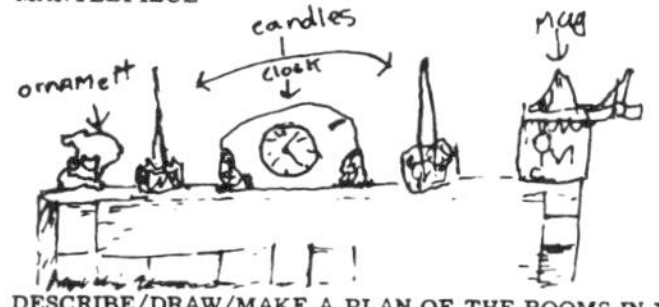

DESCRIBE/DRAW/MAKE A PLAN OF THE ROOMS IN YOUR HOUSE YOU USE TO EAT IN

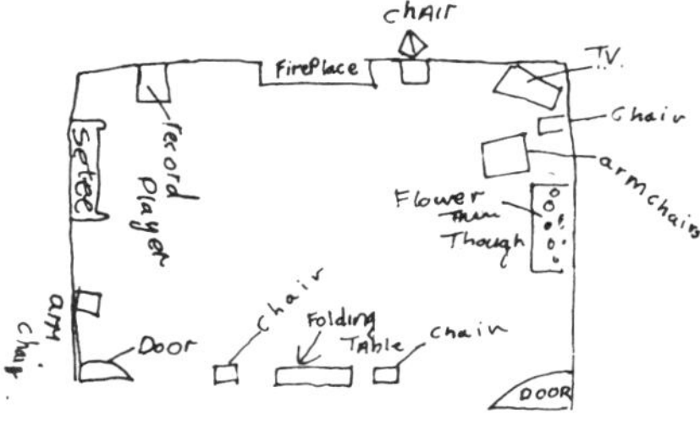

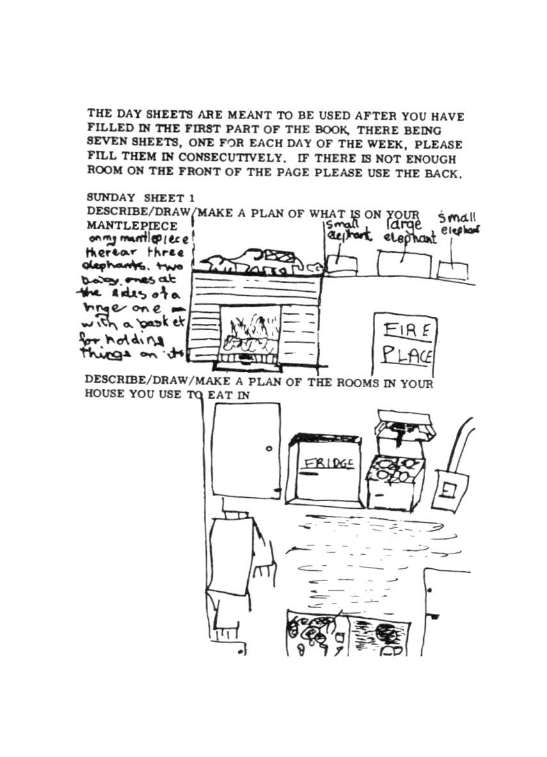

THE DAY SHEETS ARE MEANT TO BE USED AFTER YOU HAVE FILLED IN THE FIRST PART OF THE BOOK, THERE BEING SEVEN SHEETS, ONE FOR EACH DAY OF THE WEEK, PLEASE FILL THEM IN CONSECUTIVELY. IF THERE IS NOT ENOUGH ROOM ON THE FRONT OF THE PAGE PLEASE USE THE BACK.

SUNDAY SHEET 1

DESCRIBE/DRAW/MAKE A PLAN OF WHAT IS ON YOUR MANTLEPIECE

on my mantlepiece therear three elephants. two baby ones at the sides of a large one with a basket for holding things on its

DESCRIBE/DRAW/MAKE A PLAN OF THE ROOMS IN YOUR HOUSE YOU USE TO EAT IN

Project area one: Greenford

THE DAY SHEETS ARE MEANT TO BE USED AFTER YOU HAVE FILLED IN THE FIRST PART OF THE BOOK, THERE BEING SEVEN SHEETS, ONE FOR EACH DAY OF THE WEEK. PLEASE FILL THEM IN CONSECUTIVELY. IF THERE IS NOT ENOUGH ROOM ON THE FRONT OF THE PAGE PLEASE USE THE BACK.

SUNDAY SHEET 1

DESCRIBE/DRAW/MAKE A PLAN OF WHAT IS ON YOUR MANTLEPIECE

IN MIDDLE IS AN OIL PAINTING OF A ROSE, PAINTED BY A FRIEND.
THERE ARE SIX ORNAMENTS, THREE EITHER SIDE OF THIS PICTURE.
THEY ARE ALL SOUVENIRS OF HOLIDAYS TAKEN BY A MEMBER OF MY FAMILY OR ELSE GIVEN BY A FRIEND.

DESCRIBE/DRAW/MAKE A PLAN OF THE ROOMS IN YOUR HOUSE YOU USE TO EAT IN

WE USUALLY EAT IN OUR SMALL SITTING ROOM. THERE IS A PIANO IN IT, ONE GATE-LEGGED TABLE, A LARGE SIDE-BOARD, AND A CABINET CONTAINING MUSIC AND BOOKS.
NEEDLESS TO SAY, THERE IS NOT MUCH SPACE IN THIS ROOM.
WE HAVE BREAKFAST IN THE KITCHEN, WHICH IS VERY SMALL.
IT IS LONG AND NARROW, WITH THE USUAL FITTINGS.

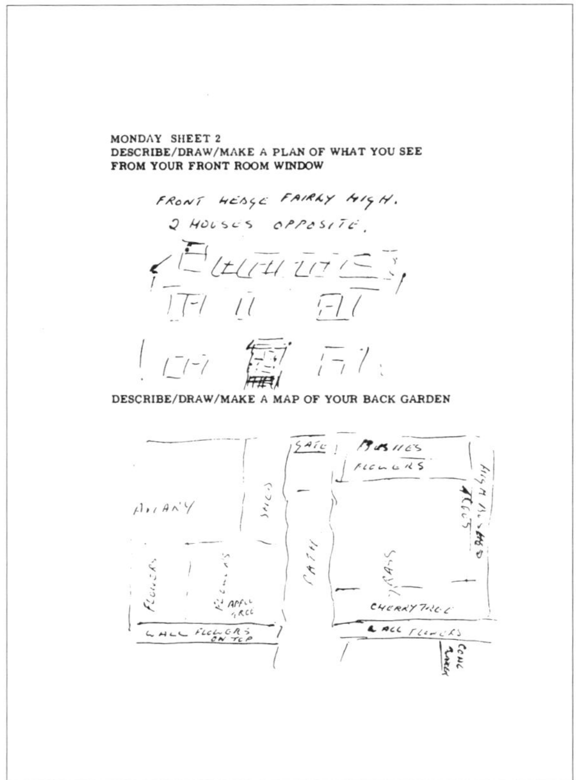

MONDAY SHEET 2
DESCRIBE/DRAW/MAKE A PLAN OF WHAT YOU SEE FROM YOUR FRONT ROOM WINDOW

FRONT HEDGE FAIRLY HIGH.
2 HOUSES OPPOSITE.

DESCRIBE/DRAW/MAKE A MAP OF YOUR BACK GARDEN

Project area one: Greenford

FRIDAY SHEET 6
DRAW/DESCRIBE YOUR IDEAL FORM OF TRANSPORT

MY IDEAL FORM OF TRANSPORT IS MY CAR – ALTHOUGH IT WOULD BE MORE PLEASANT TO TRAVEL IF MOST OF THE TRAFFIC COULD BE REMOVED!

DRAW/DESCRIBE/MAKE A MAP OF YOUR IDEAL HOUSE

SPACIOUS ROOMS, WITH A LOT OF WINDOWS. CENTRALLY HEATED. ENOUGH ROOM TO ACCOMODATE MY FAMILY EASILY (ie. A SITTING ROOM FOR EVERY MEMBER OF THE FAMILY).
IT WOULD ALSO MAKE LIFE EASIER, IF THE BATH AND TOILET WERE IN SEPARATE ROOMS!

FRIDAY SHEET 6
DRAW/DESCRIBE YOUR IDEAL FORM OF TRANSPORT

WALKING IF POSSIBLE
OTHERWISE TRAIN - NOT UNDERGROUND

DRAW/DESCRIBE/MAKE A MAP OF YOUR IDEAL HOUSE

MY IDEAL HOUSE WOULD BE
WITH THE GARDEN IN THE MIDDLE
ALSO LARGE GROUNDS ROUND THE OUTSIDE

GDN

MADE OF RED BRICK

DOWNSTAIRS
DINING ROOM
DRAWING ROOM
LIBRARY - MUSIC ROOM
KITCHEN
BATHROOM
SCULLERY
UPSTAIRS
2 BATHROOMS
4 BEDROOMS

Project area one: Greenford

ON THE INCOMPLETE DATA SHEET AT THE BACK OF THE MANUAL ARE A SERIES OF INCOMPLETE OBJECTS/PHOTOGRAPHS LETTERED A-P: CAN YOU IDENTIFY THE COMPLETE OBJECT/PHOTOGRAPH FROM THE COMPLETE DATA SHEETS RECORDING THE SHEET NUMBER AND LETTER. THEN CAN YOU DESCRIBE ASSOCIATIONS THAT YOU HAVE WITH THE COMPLETE OBJECT/PHOTOGRAPH.

INCOMPLETE OBJECT A
COMPLETE OBJECT SHEET NO. 1 OBJECT LETTER. I
DESCRIBE YOUR ASSOCIATIONS.

INCOMPLETE OBJECT B
COMPLETE OBJECT SHEET NO. 2 OBJECT LETTER. A
DESCRIBE YOUR ASSOCIATIONS. Unhappy!
For us this was the house that got away. Owner changed mind thank God!

INCOMPLETE OBJECT C
COMPLETE OBJECT SHEET NO. 1 OBJECT LETTER. B
DESCRIBE YOUR ASSOCIATIONS. !
DO IT YOURSELF!

INCOMPLETE OBJECT D
COMPLETE OBJECT SHEET NO. 2 OBJECT LETTER. D
DESCRIBE YOUR ASSOCIATIONS.
MOCK TUDOR BANK MANAGER (SUBURBAN) TYPE

INCOMPLETE OBJECT E
COMPLETE OBJECT SHEET NO. 2 OBJECT LETTER. J
DESCRIBE YOUR ASSOCIATIONS. THE ONCE A YEAR TRIP TO BRIGHTON WITH THE KIDS. FOR THE REST OF THE YEAR – THANK HEAVEN FOR MINIS.

INCOMPLETE OBJECT F
COMPLETE OBJECT SHEET NO. 2 OBJECT LETTER. H
DESCRIBE YOUR ASSOCIATIONS. BET THEY DON'T HAVE GREENFLY OR KIDS THAT GET DIRTY

WITH PHOTOGRAPH D DESCRIBE WHAT KIND OF PHANTASY PROJECTION YOU ASSOCIATE THIS FEATURE WITH.........
WHEN SHE LOCKS HIM OUT HE SPENDS THE NIGHT ON THE BENCH

DESCRIBE WHAT FUNCTION THE OBJECTS THAT MAKE UP E HAVE... ONE DAY THEY WILL PLANT TWO CLIMBING PLANTS AND THE HANGING BASKET WILL BE FILLED WITH GERANIUMS AND TRAILING LOBELIA

DESCRIBE WHAT SOCIAL ROLE F HAS.....................
USEFUL TO PEEP THROUGH WITHOUT BEING SEEN

DESCRIPTION SHEET NO 2

WHAT SOCIAL FUNCTION DOES A HAVE....................
THE CHILDREN CAN CLIMB TOGETHER

DESCRIBE WHAT B MEANS IN YOUR NEIGHBOURHOOD........
ONE SIDE ROAD LEADING INTO ANOTHER

DESCRIBE WHAT FUNCTION YOU THINK A FRONT GATE HAS
IT KEEPS MY DOG IN AND THEIR DOGS OUT

WHAT SOCIAL DISPLAY FUNCTION DOES D HAVE...........
IT IS PLEASANT TO LOOK AT AS ONE WALKS PAST

DESCRIBE THE ROLE E HAS IN AFFECTING THE SOCIAL BEHAVIOUR OF WEST LONDON............................
ENCOURAGES COMMUTERS TO CLUTTER UP OUR ROADS WITH PARKED CARS

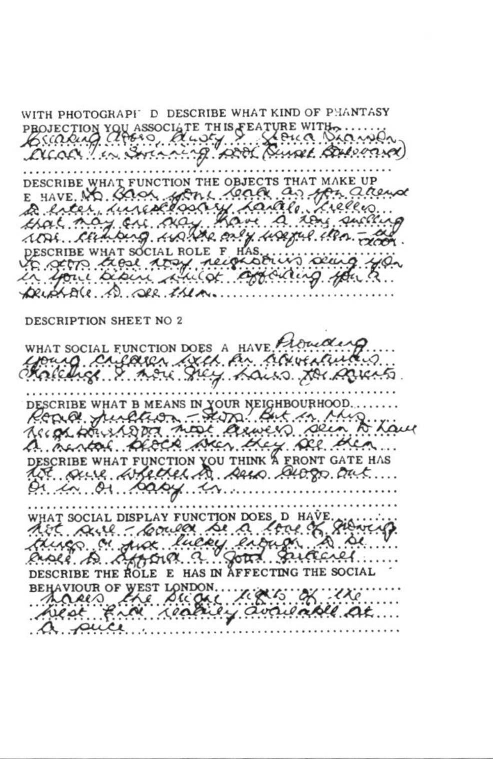

WITH PHOTOGRAPH D DESCRIBE WHAT KIND OF PHANTASY PROJECTION YOU ASSOCIATE THIS FEATURE WITH. Breaking Apart, Dusty & Gloria Swanson dead in swimming pool (Sunset Boulevard)

DESCRIBE WHAT FUNCTION THE OBJECTS THAT MAKE UP E HAVE. To bash your leg as you attend & enter, unnecessary handle, trellis that may one day have a rose swelling [illegible] climbing walls the only useful item – the door.

DESCRIBE WHAT SOCIAL ROLE F HAS. To stop those nosy neighbours seeing you in your bikini without affording you the privilege to see them.

DESCRIPTION SHEET NO 2

WHAT SOCIAL FUNCTION DOES A HAVE. Providing young children with an adventurous challenge & more grey hairs for parents.

DESCRIBE WHAT B MEANS IN YOUR NEIGHBOURHOOD. Road junction – Stop! But in this neighbourhood most drivers seem to have a mental block when they see them.

DESCRIBE WHAT FUNCTION YOU THINK A FRONT GATE HAS. Not sure whether to keep dogs out or in or baby in.

WHAT SOCIAL DISPLAY FUNCTION DOES D HAVE. Not sure – could be a love of growing things or just lucky enough to be able to afford a good gardener.

DESCRIBE THE ROLE E HAS IN AFFECTING THE SOCIAL BEHAVIOUR OF WEST LONDON. Makes the bright lights of the West End readily available at a price.

WITH PHOTOGRAPH D DESCRIBE WHAT KIND OF PHANTASY PROJECTION YOU ASSOCIATE THIS FEATURE WITH........ [illegible]

DESCRIBE WHAT FUNCTION THE OBJECTS THAT MAKE UP E HAVE... [illegible]

DESCRIBE WHAT SOCIAL ROLE F HAS.. [illegible]

DESCRIPTION SHEET NO 2

WHAT SOCIAL FUNCTION DOES A HAVE.. [illegible]

DESCRIBE WHAT B MEANS IN YOUR NEIGHBOURHOOD........ [illegible]

DESCRIBE WHAT FUNCTION YOU THINK A FRONT GATE HAS [illegible]

WHAT SOCIAL DISPLAY FUNCTION DOES D HAVE... [illegible]

DESCRIBE THE ROLE E HAS IN AFFECTING THE SOCIAL BEHAVIOUR OF WEST LONDON.... [illegible]

Project area two: Osterley

THE DAY SHEETS ARE MEANT TO BE USED AFTER YOU AVE FILLED IN THE FIRST PART OF THE BOOK, THERE BEING SEVEN SHEETS, ONE FOR EACH DAY OF THE WEEK, PLEASE FILL THEM IN CONSECUTIVELY. IF THERE IS NOT ENOUGH ROOM ON THE FRONT OF THE PAGE PLEASE USE THE BACK.

SUNDAY SHEET 1
DESCRIBE/DRAW/MAKE A PLAN OF WHAT IS ON YOUR MANTLEPIECE

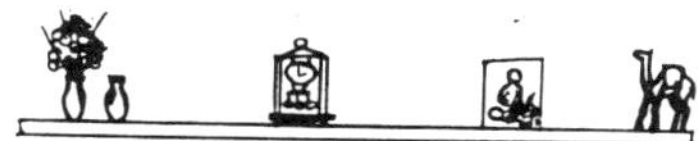

DESCRIBE/DRAW/MAKE A PLAN OF THE ROOMS IN YOUR HOUSE YOU USE TO EAT IN

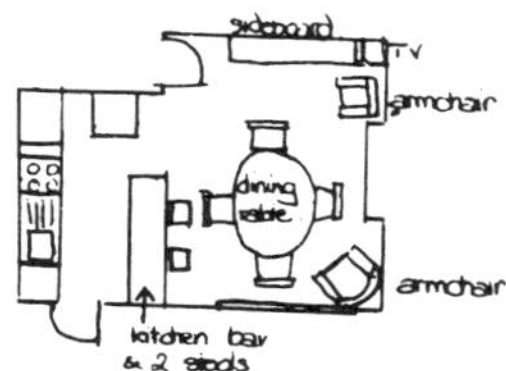

MONDAY SHEET 2
DESCRIBE/DRAW/MAKE A PLAN OF WHAT YOU SEE
FROM YOUR FRONT ROOM WINDOW

LOOKING LEFT:— CARS, ROSES NEXT DOOR
HOUSES OVER THE ROAD, CURTAINS DRAWN CLOSED
ONE MAN IN HIS GARDEN WORKING TREES.
LOOKING CENTRE:— OUR ROSES, OUR CAR
HOUSE OVER THE ROAD CURTAINS DRAWN CLOSED

LOOKING RIGHT:— OUR ROSES, CARS, HOUSE
OVER ROAD CURTAINS CLOSED NEXT DOORS
ROSES, CARS. IN THE DISTANCE - CARS
CARAVAN HOUSES WITH CURTAINS DRAWN
CLOSED STREET LAMP, TREES CARS
AIRCRAFT IN THE SKY APPROACHING HEATHROW

DESCRIBE/DRAW/MAKE A MAP OF YOUR BACK GARDEN

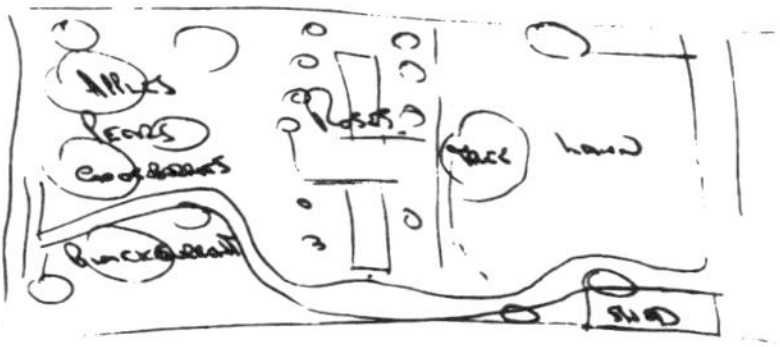

Project area two: Osterley

WEDNESDAY SHEET 4

DESCRIBE/DRAW/MAKE A MAP OF YOUR STREET

Tree lined road

passage to station

tube line

Station

DESCRIBE/DRAW/MAKE A MAP OF THE MOST OUTSTANDING FEATURE IN YOUR NEIGHBOURHOOD

Osterley Park

This Park is within a ¼ mile & covers a large area, two lakes, Osterley House, (open to visitors) tea room. Dogs allowed only on a lead. Car park.

Very crowded not weekends.

WEDNESDAY SHEET 4
DESCRIBE/DRAW/MAKE A MAP OF YOUR STREET

The Street Is A Cul De Sac Lined With
Three & Four Bedroomed Semi-Detached Houses
In Good Repair - Built Around 1935 Some
Of A Similar Design About 1950. Trees On
Both Sides Of Street. The Street Has
A Large Population Of Cars Mainly By
People Who Use The Train To The City.
Most Gardens In The Front Are Small
Neat With A Lawn, Roses, Most Houses
Have Garages With Shared Drives Between
The Houses. House Colours Vary As Do
The House Designs In A Limited Way
Predominant Colours White Green Black Yellow

DESCRIBE/DRAW/MAKE A MAP OF THE MOST OUTSTANDING
FEATURE IN YOUR NEIGHBOURHOOD

Heathrow Airport.

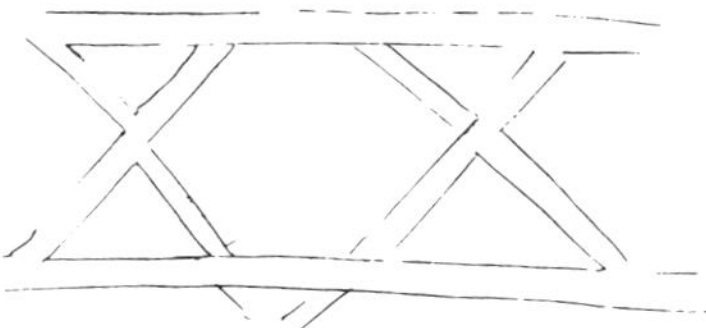

Project area two: Osterley

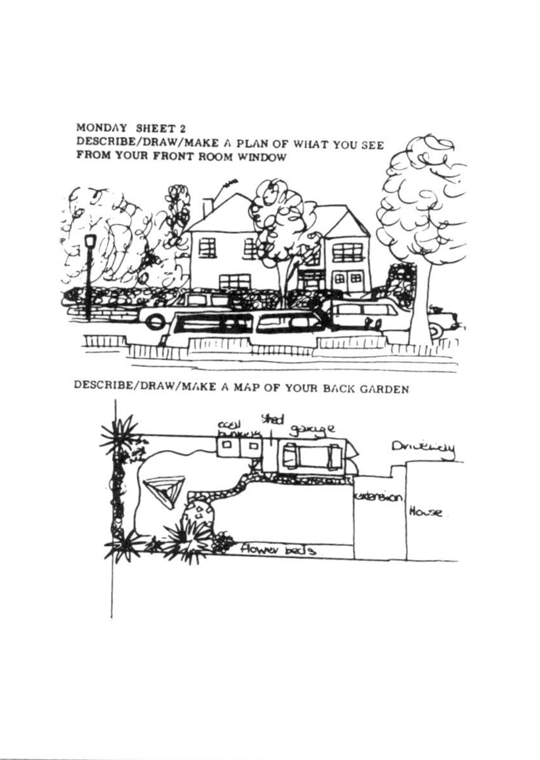
MONDAY SHEET 2
DESCRIBE/DRAW/MAKE A PLAN OF WHAT YOU SEE FROM YOUR FRONT ROOM WINDOW
DESCRIBE/DRAW/MAKE A MAP OF YOUR BACK GARDEN
coal bunkers
shed
garage
Driveway
extension
House
flower beds

TUESDAY SHEET 3

DESCRIBE YESTERDAY'S ROUTINE

AWOKE 6-30 AM, MADE TEA, WALKED TO STATION TO BUY PAPERS. RETURNED READ F. TIMES DRANK TEA. LEFT IN CAR AT 8-15 FOR ENFIELD VIA NORTH CIRCULAR ARRIVED 9-30 WORKED UNTIL 1-15. DROVE TO PUB WITH FRIEND HAD BEER & MEAT ROLLS. RETURNED TO ENFIELD. DROVE TO TOTTENHAM 2-30 LEFT TOTTENHAM 5-30 RETURNED HOME VIA N. CIRCULAR. RETURNED 6-25 PM. READ EVENING STANDARD FOR 30 MINS. AFTER PLAYED 'WAR' WITH SON WHILST WAITING FOR EVENING MEAL. — EAT MEAL PLAYED CARS WITH 4 YEAR OLD SON AGAIN UNTIL HIS BEDTIME. WATCHED T.V DROPPED OFF TO SLEEP FOR 1/2 HOUR. MORE TEA AT 10-45PM BED 11-30PM

DESCRIBE YOUR LEISURE ROUTINES

EVERY MORNING I CHART A SELECTED NUMBER OF SHARES. THIS IS MY ONLY DAILY ROUTINE. A WEEKLY ROUTINE IS A FRIDAY STUDY OF RACING FORM FOR SATURDAY RACING. — NONE ROUTINE LEISURE AND BY THAT I MEAN I HAVE NO SPECIFIED TIMES. IS GARDENING, READING FINANCIAL NEWS, REPORTS & PAPERS AT RANDOM. T.V. VIEWING AGAIN AT RANDOM. VISITS TO PARKS, MOTHER-IN-LAW SHOPPING. PLAYING GAMES WITH SON AND ATTEMPT AT TUITION

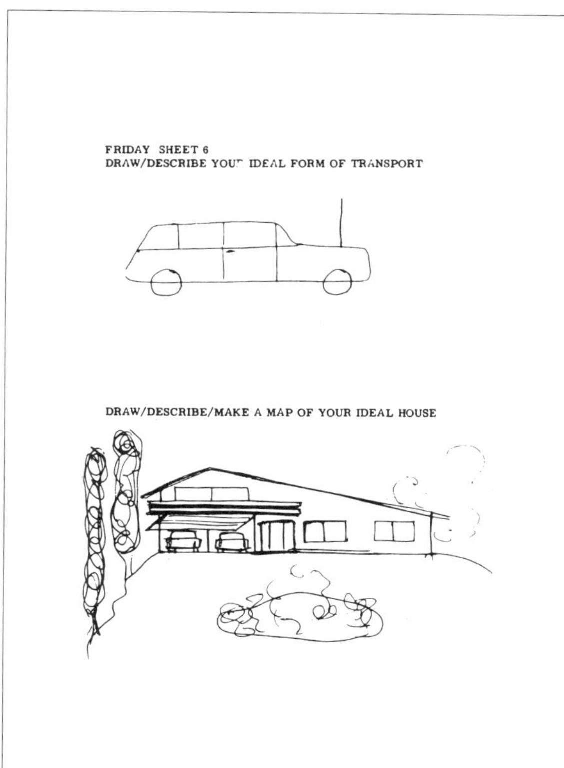
FRIDAY SHEET 6
DRAW/DESCRIBE YOUR IDEAL FORM OF TRANSPORT

DRAW/DESCRIBE/MAKE A MAP OF YOUR IDEAL HOUSE

SATURDAY SHEET 7
DRAW/DESCRIBE/MAKE A MAP OF YOUR IDEAL GARDEN

An informal garden mainly lawn evergreen trees & plants A few fruit trees, plenty of room for children to play on patio area Flowering Shrubs that dont need too much attention.

DESCRIBE YOUR IDEAL EXISTENCE

I could dream of an existence where a housekeeper does all the chores in the house, the washing, ironing, cleaning & I would be left to do the cooking, looking after the children, entertaining though after a while I expect I would become bored.

This kind of existence would be ideal in a hot climate living in a house with swimming pool in garden & being able to sun bathe & have drinks on terrace each afternoon! (I wouldnt even want to do the cooking then)!!

ON THE INCOMPLETE DATA SHEET AT THE BACK OF THE MANUAL ARE A SERIES OF INCOMPLETE OBJECTS/PHOTOGRAPHS LETTERED A-P: CAN YOU IDENTIFY THE COMPLETE OBJECT/PHOTOGRAPH FROM THE COMPLETE DATA SHEETS RECORDING THE SHEET NUMBER AND LETTER. THEN CAN YOU DESCRIBE ASSOCIATIONS THAT YOU HAVE WITH THE COMPLETE OBJECT/PHOTOGRAPH.

INCOMPLETE OBJECT A
COMPLETE OBJECT SHEET NO. 1 OBJECT LETTER. A
DESCRIBE YOUR ASSOCIATIONS.
This looks like a fairy
garden gate

INCOMPLETE OBJECT B
COMPLETE OBJECT SHEET NO. 1 OBJECT LETTER. G
DESCRIBE YOUR ASSOCIATIONS. To look through and
[illegible] a wide window
not like the windows in our House

INCOMPLETE OBJECT C
COMPLETE OBJECT SHEET NO. 1 OBJECT LETTER. C
DESCRIBE YOUR ASSOCIATIONS. a fence
usaly to Devide Property

INCOMPLETE OBJECT D
COMPLETE OBJECT SHEET NO. 1 OBJECT LETTER. D
DESCRIBE YOUR ASSOCIATIONS. front of Roof
of House

INCOMPLETE OBJECT E
COMPLETE OBJECT SHEET NO. 1 OBJECT LETTER. E
DESCRIBE YOUR ASSOCIATIONS. Road Sign
To go Straight on

INCOMPLETE OBJECT F
COMPLETE OBJECT SHEET NO. 1 OBJECT LETTER. F
DESCRIBE YOUR ASSOCIATIONS. To Sit on
Bench

Project area three: Hanwell

ON THE INCOMPLETE DATA SHEET AT THE BACK OF THE MANUAL ARE A SERIES OF INCOMPLETE OBJECTS/PHOTOGRAPHS LETTERED A-P: CAN YOU IDENTIFY THE COMPLETE OBJECT/PHOTOGRAPH FROM THE COMPLETE DATA SHEETS RECORDING THE SHEET NUMBER AND LETTER. THEN CAN YOU DESCRIBE ASSOCIATIONS THAT YOU HAVE WITH THE COMPLETE OBJECT/PHOTOGRAPH.

INCOMPLETE OBJECT A
COMPLETE OBJECT SHEET NO. . 1 . . . OBJECT LETTER I . . .
DESCRIBE YOUR ASSOCIATIONS. . . [illegible], MIDDLE . [illegible] . . . [illegible] . . . [illegible] . . . .
INCOMPLETE OBJECT B
COMPLETE OBJECT SHEET NO. . 2 . . OBJECT LETTER. A . . .
DESCRIBE YOUR ASSOCIATIONS. . . MIDDLE . CLASS . . . FAMILY . , . . OLD . STYLE . . WINDOWS . . . .
INCOMPLETE OBJECT C
COMPLETE OBJECT SHEET NO. . 1 . . . OBJECT LETTER. . B . .
DESCRIBE YOUR ASSOCIATIONS. . UNIFORM . SCHOOL . . TYPE . . GATE . . (FRONT) . . . .
INCOMPLETE OBJECT D
COMPLETE OBJECT SHEET NO. . 2 . . OBJECT LETTER. . D . .
DESCRIBE YOUR ASSOCIATIONS. . . OLD . . . FASHIONED . HOUSE . . . WHICH . . HAS . BEEN . . . MODERNISED . . . . ABOUT . . . 5 . . . YEARS . . . AGO . . .
INCOMPLETE OBJECT E
COMPLETE OBJECT SHEET NO. . 2 . . OBJECT LETTER. . J . .
DESCRIBE YOUR ASSOCIATIONS. . . . SIGN . . . POST . . . IN . THE . . MIDDLE . . OF . . . AN . . . OLD . . . HOUSING . ESTATE . . . .
INCOMPLETE OBJECT F
COMPLETE OBJECT SHEET NO. . 2 . OBJECT LETTER. . . H . .
DESCRIBE YOUR ASSOCIATIONS. . . PRIVATELY . . OWNED . . HOUSE . . . IN . . A . . . . RURAL . . . DISTRICT . . . .

THE DAY SHEETS ARE MEANT TO BE USED AFTER YOU HAVE FILLED IN THE FIRST PART OF THE BOOK, THERE BEING SEVEN SHEETS, ONE FOR EACH DAY OF THE WEEK, PLEASE FILL THEM IN CONSECUTIVELY. IF THERE IS NOT ENOUGH ROOM ON THE FRONT OF THE PAGE PLEASE USE THE BACK.

SUNDAY SHEET 1

DESCRIBE/DRAW/MAKE A PLAN OF WHAT IS ON YOUR MANTLEPIECE 2 PLASTIC ELEPHANTS, 1 WHITE & 1 GREY
2 SMALLER " " , " "
2 WHITE " GIRAFFES, 1 ON ITS SIDE
APPROX 4 LETTERS
1 PEWTER JUG, WITH A PEN STICKING OUT THE TOP. THE JUG IS ON THE LETTERS, AND THERE ARE ODDS & SODS IN THE JUG.

DESCRIBE/DRAW/MAKE A PLAN OF THE ROOMS IN YOUR HOUSE YOU USE TO EAT IN

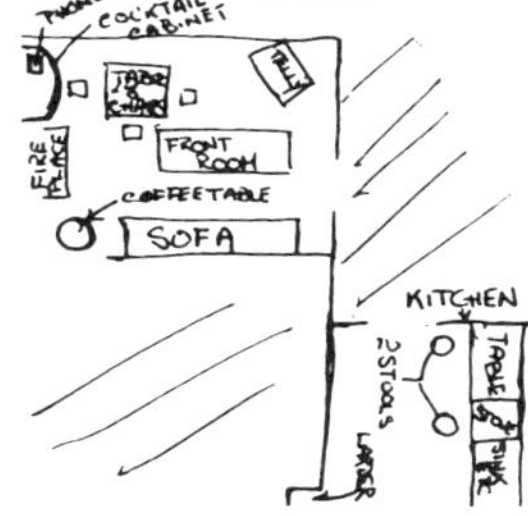

MONDAY SHEET 2
DESCRIBE/DRAW/MAKE A PLAN OF WHAT YOU SEE
FROM YOUR FRONT ROOM WINDOW

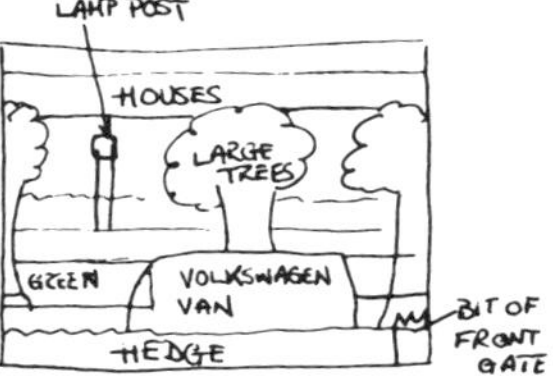

DESCRIBE/DRAW/MAKE A MAP OF YOUR BACK GARDEN

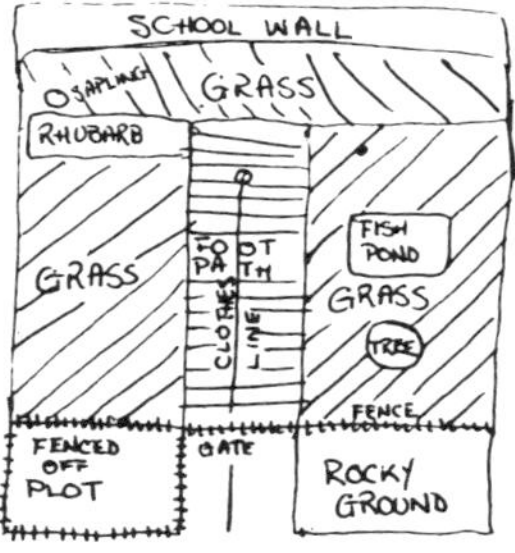

Project area three: Hanwell

WITH PHOTOGRAPH D DESCRIBE WHAT KIND OF PHANTASY PROJECTION YOU ASSOCIATE THIS FEATURE WITH.

SOMEONE WITH RELIGIOUS BACKGROUND OR WHO LIKES OLD FASHIONED THINGS

DESCRIBE WHAT FUNCTION THE OBJECTS THAT MAKE UP E HAVE. TRELLIS FOR CLIMBING PLANTS

HANGING BASKET FOR FLOWERS

DESCRIBE WHAT SOCIAL ROLE F HAS. TO GIVE YOU PRIVACY IN YOUR GARDEN

DESCRIPTION SHEET NO 2

WHAT SOCIAL FUNCTION DOES A HAVE. ADVENTURE PLAY GROUND

DESCRIBE WHAT B MEANS IN YOUR NEIGHBOURHOOD. TRAFFIC COMING UP TO DOUBLE LINES TO STOP FOR TRAFFIC ON CROSS ROAD.

DESCRIBE WHAT FUNCTION YOU THINK A FRONT GATE HAS

KEEPS OUT DOGS & CHILDREN THIS

KEEPING FRONT OF HOUSE TIDY

WHAT SOCIAL DISPLAY FUNCTION DOES D HAVE. AS THIS LOOKS LIKE A PRIVATE GARDEN PRESUMABLY FOR OWNER'S ENJOYMENT & SHOWING TO FRIENDS

DESCRIBE THE ROLE E HAS IN AFFECTING THE SOCIAL BEHAVIOUR OF WEST LONDON. ROLE TO GO QUICKLY EITHER TO TOWN OR OUT IN THE COUNTRY

THE DAY SHEETS ARE MEANT TO BE USED AFTER YOU HAVE FILLED IN THE FIRST PART OF THE BOOK, THERE BEING SEVEN SHEETS, ONE FOR EACH DAY OF THE WEEK. PLEASE FILL THEM IN CONSECUTIVELY. IF THERE IS NOT ENOUGH ROOM ON THE FRONT OF THE PAGE PLEASE USE THE BACK.

SUNDAY SHEET 1

DESCRIBE/DRAW/MAKE A PLAN OF WHAT IS ON YOUR MANTLEPIECE

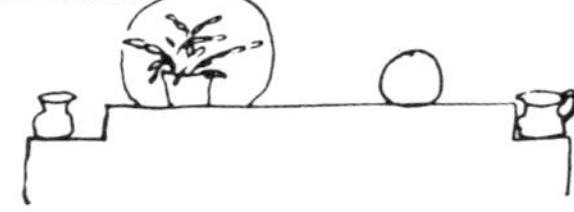

DESCRIBE/DRAW/MAKE A PLAN OF THE ROOMS IN YOUR HOUSE YOU USE TO EAT IN

we use the living room to eat in

Project area three: Hanwell

MONDAY SHEET 2
DESCRIBE/DRAW/MAKE A PLAN OF WHAT YOU SEE
FROM YOUR FRONT ROOM WINDOW

BLOCK OF TWO STOREY FLATS
SIMILAR TO MY OWN BLOCK

DESCRIBE/DRAW/MAKE A MAP OF YOUR BACK GARDEN

1 BED OF MINIATURE ROSES
2 BIRD BATH
3 " TABLE

TUESDAY SHEET 3

DESCRIBE YESTERDAY'S ROUTINE

UP AT 7 AM. FED ANIMAL + PREPARED FOOD FOR SAME DURING DAY. HAD BREAKFAST, SPOT OF HOUSEWORK, THEN 3 TRAINS TO KNIGHTSBRIDGE WHERE WORK. OUT LUNCHTIME SHOPPING. HOME IN EVENING GOT MEAL DID SOME GARDENING PREPARED FOOD FOR ANIMAL'S BREAKFAST WATCHED T.V.

DESCRIBE YOUR LEISURE ROUTINES

CHIEFLY GARDENING AT MOMENT

OCCASIONAL VISIT TO THEATRE

Project area three: Hanwell

'EDNESDAY SHEET 4

'ESCRIBE/DRAW/MAKE A MAP OF YOUR STREET

SHOPS HOUSES CHURCH WASTE GROUND ENTRANCE TO NURSERY SCHOOL HOUSE FLATS HOUSES HOUSES HOUSES FLATS HOUSES HOUSES

HOUSES HOUSES HOUSES FLATS HOUSES HOUSES FLATS HOUSES HOUSES FLATS HOUSES HOUSES

ALL HOUSES HAVE OWN FRONT GARDENS. FLATS (2 STOREY) HAVE GRASS IN FRONT. SOME CORNERS HAVE BUSHES & SOME HAVE GRASS. TREES PLANTED BY COUNCIL IN SOME GARDENS & CORNER

'ESCRIBE/DRAW/MAKE A MAP OF THE MOST OUTSTANDING 'EATURE IN YOUR NEIGHBOURHOOD

THE CLOCK TOWER OF THE CUCKOO ESTATE COMMUNITY CENTRE.

THURSDAY SHEET 5

DRAW/DESCRIBE A TYPICAL PERSON IN YOUR NEIGHBOURHOOD

MORE THAN LIKELY PART
IRISH – ALTHOUGH POSSIBLY
WEST INDIAN – 2 OR 3
CHILDREN, LIKELY TO BE
TEENAGERS – MANUAL
JOB FOR DAD – MOTHER
POSSIBLY WORKING –
1 CAR – BRITISH FAMILY
SALOON – 3 CHANNEL
T.V. NOT COLOUR –
READS DAILY MIRROR OR
SUN – KIDS STAND
AROUND OUTSIDE
LOCAL PUB NOTHING
TO DO – EAT WELL,
EVERY DAY – NOT TOO
BOTHERED ABOUT KEEPING
UP WITH THE JONESES.

WHAT COLOUR DO YOU ASSOCIATE WITH THE FOLLOWING AREAS ON THE PROJECT MAP:

AREA ONE YELLOW OR GREY AREA TWO

AREA THREE BLUE AREA FOUR

DESCRIBE/DRAW/MAKE A PLAN OF WHAT YOU IMAGINE TO BE A TYPICAL HOUSE FROM THE FOLLOWING AREAS ON THE PROJECT MAP

AREA ONE AREA TWO

AREA THREE AREA FOUR

FRONT ~~BACK~~ BEDROOMS

SMALL BEDROOM

FRONT BEDROOM ABOVE FRONT ROOM

BACK BEDROOM ABOVE LOUNGE

BACK BEDROOM

BATH W/C

BATH & W/C ABOVE KITCHEN

Project area three: Hanwell

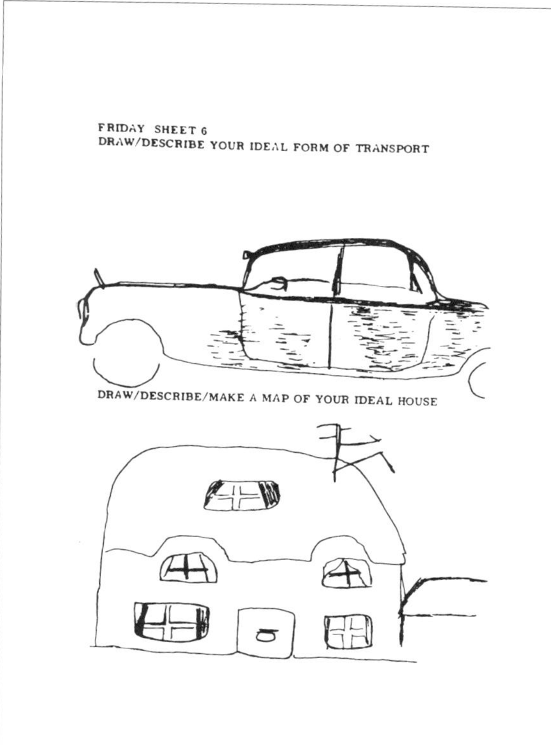
FRIDAY SHEET 6
DRAW/DESCRIBE YOUR IDEAL FORM OF TRANSPORT
DRAW/DESCRIBE/MAKE A MAP OF YOUR IDEAL HOUSE

SATURDAY SHEET 7
DRAW/DESCRIBE/MAKE A MAP OF YOUR IDEAL GARDEN

AN INFORMAL COUNTRY TYPE GARDEN BUT
DEFINITELY BIG ENOUGH FOR SOME TREES
IF I HAVE TO LOOK AFTER IT MYSELF.
OTHERWISE A LANDSCAPE GARDEN, COMBINING BOTH
INFORMAL + FORMAL, WITH BEAUTIFUL LAWNS
AND LOVELY BIG TREES

DESCRIBE YOUR IDEAL EXISTENCE

INTERESTING PART TIME JOB AS AT PRESENT.
NOT TOO MUCH HOUSEWORK, LEAVING TIME FOR
GARDENING, VISITING, AND GOING TO THEATRE,
PLACES OF INTEREST ETC.

Project area three: Hanwell

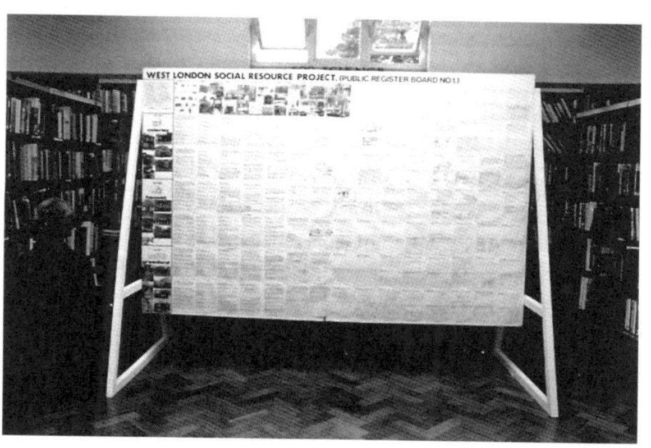

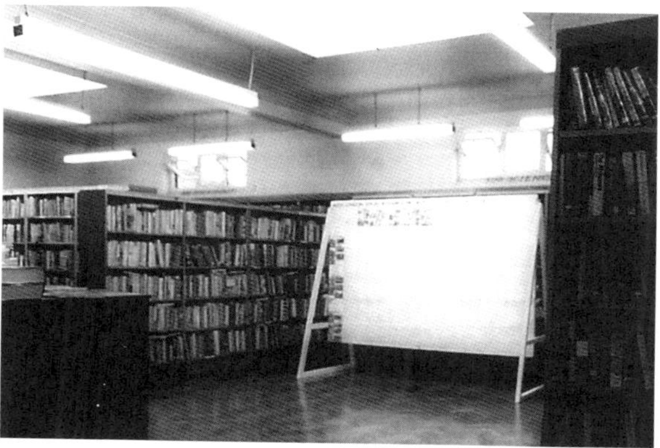

FIGURE 13 Public register board no. 1. Situated in a branch library adjacent to one of the project areas. This board displayed participant returns from the West London Manual.

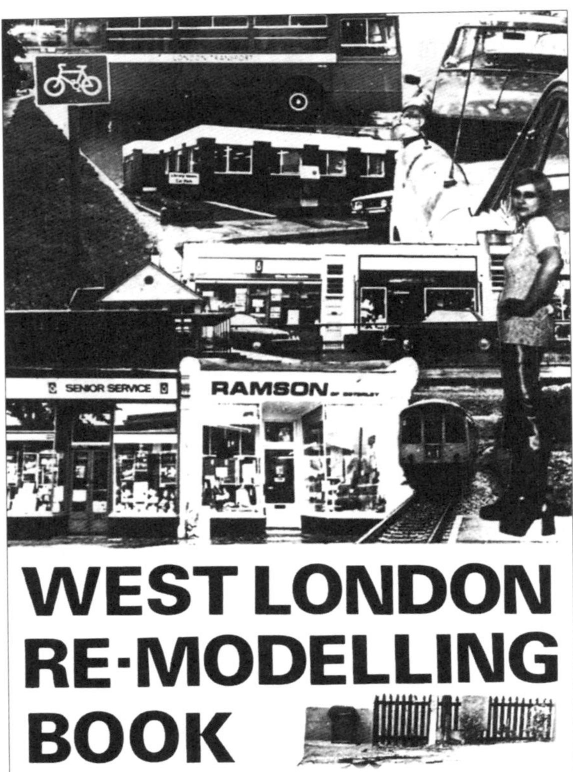

FIGURE 14 The front cover of the West London Re-modelling Book. Neighbourhood items taken from the project areas are depicted: for example, the library is the one at Osterley used in the project.

FIGURE 15 West London Re-modelling Book.
The following pages show examples of participant returns.

h

SHEET TWO

DESCRIBE WHAT SOCIAL/PHYSICAL NEEDS THE HOUSE YOU LIVE IN FULLFILLS.

Socially - A place to entertain our friends
Physical needs - Security - an anchor
comfort - warmth. To be able to create
in the home - personal artistic ability. In
fact to be an individual within a family
unit.

DESCRIBE, DRAW, MAKE A MAP OF WHAT CHANGES IF ANY COULD BE MADE TO THE INTERIOR OF THE HOUSE YOU LIVE IN, SHOWING HOW THEY RELATE TO THE NEEDS IT FULLFILLS.

EXTENSION BECOMES KITCHEN

KITCHEN

EXTEND LOUNGE

LOUNGE

STAIRS

FRONT DOOR

Project area one: Greenford

O

SHEET TWO

DESCRIBE WHAT SOCIAL/PHYSICAL NEEDS THE HOUSE YOU LIVE IN FULLFILLS.

WE FIND OUR HOUSE ADEQUATE [illegible] CHANGING [illegible]

[illegible]

DESCRIBE, DRAW, MAKE A MAP OF WHAT CHANGES IF ANY COULD BE MADE TO THE INTERIOR OF THE HOUSE YOU LIVE IN, SHOWING HOW THEY RELATE TO THE NEEDS IT FULLFILLS.

THE CHANGE MOST NECESSARY IS THAT THE BATHROOM SHOULD BE UPSTAIRS INSTEAD OF DOWNSTAIRS NEXT TO THE KITCHEN. IF IT WERE POSSIBLE [illegible] THE WATER PIPES I SUGGEST TO [illegible] THE LARGE BEDROOM SMALLER, [illegible] THE BATHROOM, THE SPACE DOWNSTAIRS COULD BE ADDED TO THE KITCHEN.

a

SHEET THREE

DESCRIBE WHAT SOCIAL/PHYSICAL NEEDS YOUR FRONT AND BACK GARDEN FULLFILLS.

FRONT	The front garden ~~[illegible]~~ is a huge size
BACK	The back garden just a little too small.

CONSIDERING THE NEEDS YOUR FRONT AND BACK GARDEN FULLFILLS, DRAW, DESCRIBE, MAKE A MAP OF WHAT ALTERATIONS YOU COULD MAKE TO THEM.

My front garden needs to have some of the shrubs of tree's cut down. Its a big mass of bushes at present. The back garden needs a fence, proper fence put up around it. We have no privacy in these gardens.

Project area one: Greenford

d

SHEET FIVE.

DESCRIBE, DRAW, MAKE A MAP OF HOW YOU THINK YOUR HOUSE, GARDEN ETC SHOULD RELATE TO YOUR NEIGHBOURS.

HOUSE

HOUSE

HOUSE

DESCRIBE AND MAKE A PLAN OF A GARDEN OR OPEN SPACE THAT COULD BE USED BY ALL THE PEOPLE IN YOUR NEIGHBOURHOOD SHOWING HOW IT WOULD FUNCTION.

Existing parks fullfill most needs. I would like to see, in addition to parks, open space were people could do anything they chose to do.

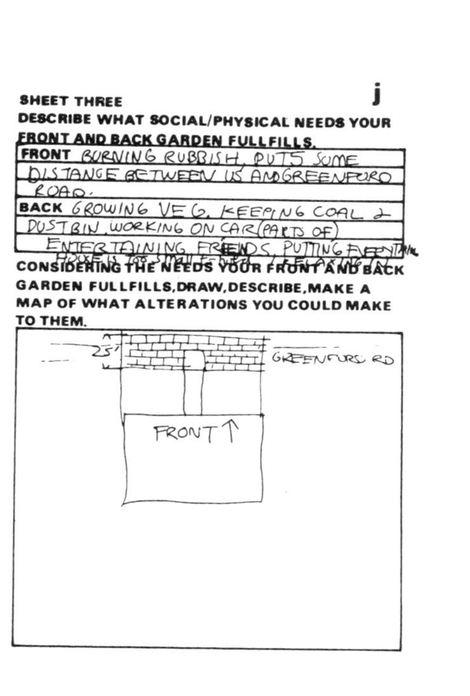

SHEET THREE **j**

DESCRIBE WHAT SOCIAL/PHYSICAL NEEDS YOUR FRONT AND BACK GARDEN FULLFILLS.

FRONT BURNING RUBBISH, PUTS SOME DISTANGE BETWEEN US ANDGREENFURD ROAD.

BACK GROWING VEG, KEEPING COAL & DUSTBIN, WORKING ON CAR (PARTS OF) ENTERTAINING FRIENDS, PUTTING EVERYTHING HOUSE IS TOO SMALL [illegible] RELAXING IN

CONSIDERING THE NEEDS YOUR FRONT AND BACK GARDEN FULLFILLS, DRAW, DESCRIBE, MAKE A MAP OF WHAT ALTERATIONS YOU COULD MAKE TO THEM.

b

SHEET THREE

DESCRIBE WHAT SOCIAL/PHYSICAL NEEDS YOUR FRONT AND BACK GARDEN FULLFILLS.

FRONT PRIVACY FROM CHILDREN AND DOGS ALLOWED TO RUN WILD

BACK PLEASANT TO SPEND TIME IN AS FORM OF GARDENING

CONSIDERING THE NEEDS YOUR FRONT AND BACK GARDEN FULLFILLS, DRAW, DESCRIBE, MAKE A MAP OF WHAT ALTERATIONS YOU COULD MAKE TO THEM.

AS WE ARE SLIGHTLY UP FROM PAVEMENT IT WOULD BE NICE TO HAVE A HEDGE INSTEAD OF IRON RAILINGS TO LOOK AT, I ALSO TO HAVE GATES WHICH WORK. THE FRONT GARDEN, OR GRASS PLOT, DOES NOT BELONG TO US, BUT THE COUNCIL.

BACK I WOULD LIKE SOLID WOODEN FENCING TO PREVENT DOGS BREAKING DOWN EXISTING WOBBLY OPEN FENCING.

SHEET SIX. **j**

MAKE A MAP OF YOUR NEIGHBOUGHOOD SHOWING HOW IT RELATES TO EXISTING SOCIAL FACILITIES, SUCH AS SHOPS, LIBRARIES, SCHOOLS, SPORTS CLUBS ETC.

STANHOPE RD

WINDMILL LANE

DAY NURSERY

SHOPS

SHOPS

BUS STOP

SHOPS

ALLOTMENTS

SCHOOL

LIBRARY CLINIC

SHOPS

SCHOOL

HOW WOULD YOU REORGANISE THE ABOVE MAP IN ORDER TO MAKE THE SOCIAL FACILITIES SERVE WHAT YOU CONSIDER YOUR NEIGHBOUGHOOD NEEDS TO BE. DESCRIBE AND DRAW A MAP.

TRAFIC

PEDESTRIANS

HOUSES

SHOP CENTRE

HOUSES

PEDESTRIANS

Project area one: Greenford

SHEET SIX. **d**

MAKE A MAP OF YOUR NEIGHBOUGHOOD SHOW-ING HOW IT RELATES TO EXISTING SOCIAL FACILITIES, SUCH AS SHOPS, LIBRARIES, SCHOOLS, SPORTS CLUBS ETC.

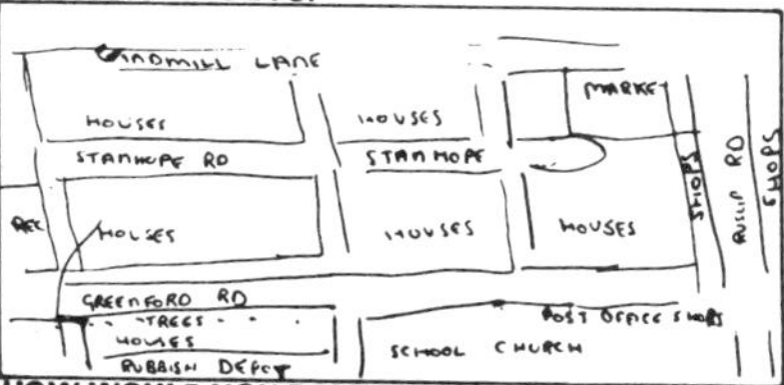

HOW WOULD YOU REORGANISE THE ABOVE MAP IN ORDER TO MAKE THE SOCIAL FACILITIES SERVE WHAT YOU CONSIDER YOUR NEIGHBOUGHOOD NEEDS TO BE. DESCRIBE AND DRAW A MAP.

MARKET

PULL DOWN THE MARKET TO MAKE WAY FOR MODERN SHOPPING PRECINCT. WITH UNDERGROUND CAR + BUS GARAGE

~~STANHOPE RD~~

BUILD GARAGES FOR TENANTS CARS TO BE RENTED BY SIDE OF RUBBISH DEPOT

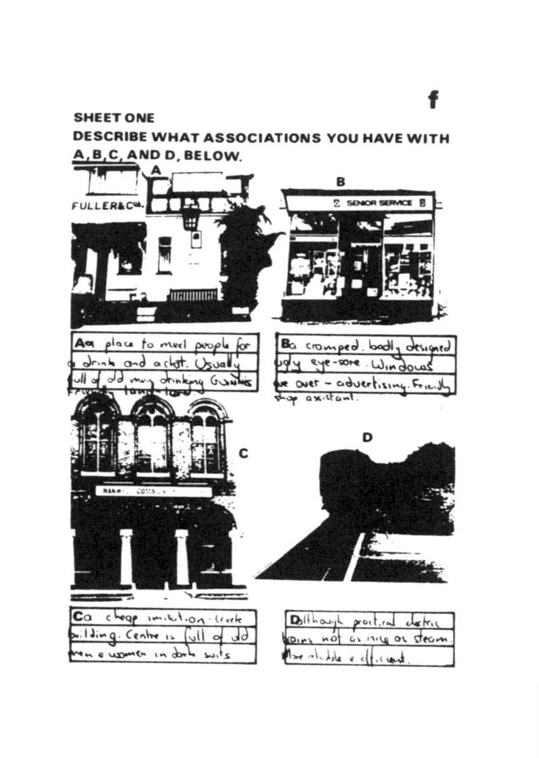

f

SHEET ONE

DESCRIBE WHAT ASSOCIATIONS YOU HAVE WITH A, B, C, AND D, BELOW.

A

B

A a place to meet people for a drink and a chat. Usually full of old men drinking Guinness

B a cramped, badly designed ugly eye-sore. Windows are over – advertising. Friendly shop assistant.

C

D

C a cheap imitation – Greek building. Centre is full of old men & women in dark suits

D although practical electric trains not as nice as steam. More reliable & efficient.

Project area two: Osterley

ambiguous – interior or exterior?

SHEET TWO

DESCRIBE WHAT SOCIAL/PHYSICAL NEEDS THE HOUSE YOU LIVE IN FULLFILLS.

Convenient for work, close to parks, library, + on main communication routes (all forms of transport). House is large enough for our family of 3, plus room to accomodate visitors several times per year. Also room to spread out + room for study.

DESCRIBE, DRAW, MAKE A MAP OF WHAT CHANGES IF ANY COULD BE MADE TO THE INTERIOR OF THE HOUSE YOU LIVE IN, SHOWING HOW THEY RELATE TO THE NEEDS IT FULLFILLS.

Removed party wall between 2 living rooms to make 1 large living room to make more use of space for 'living'.

Kitchen had a wall removed so access to sink was not impaired. Views + many cupboards installed + cooker more sensibly sited. (These alterations are still being undertaken)

cooker
cupboards
sink
wall
old
cupboards
cooker
cupboards
sink
new

Because of constant stream of visitors it is convenient to have a 'spare' bedroom. In the future a [illegible] the loft could be installed to avoid encroaching on study

k

SHEET TWO

DESCRIBE WHAT SOCIAL/PHYSICAL NEEDS THE HOUSE YOU LIVE IN FULLFILLS.

[illegible]

DESCRIBE,DRAW,MAKE A MAP OF WHAT CHANGES IF ANY COULD BE MADE TO THE INTERIOR OF THE HOUSE YOU LIVE IN,SHOWING HOW THEY RELATE TO THE NEEDS IT FULLFILLS.

[illegible]

Project area two: Osterley

f

SHEET THREE

DESCRIBE WHAT SOCIAL/PHYSICAL NEEDS YOUR FRONT AND BACK GARDEN FULLFILLS.

FRONT Merely a space separating us from the passers by

BACK Useful in summer for enjoying fine weather picnics. Useful means of exercising by car cleaning

CONSIDERING THE NEEDS YOUR FRONT AND BACK GARDEN FULLFILLS, DRAW, DESCRIBE, MAKE A MAP OF WHAT ALTERATIONS YOU COULD MAKE TO THEM.

wall

Open plan by knocking down wall

k

SHEET FIVE.

DESCRIBE, DRAW, MAKE A MAP OF HOW YOU THINK YOUR HOUSE, GARDEN ETC SHOULD RELATE TO YOUR NEIGHBOURS.

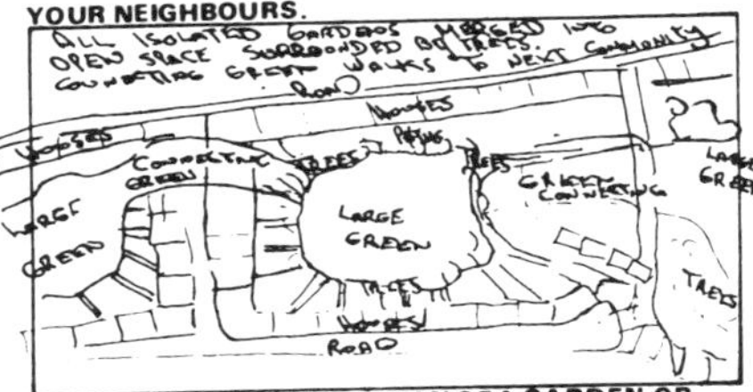

DESCRIBE AND MAKE A PLAN OF A GARDEN OR OPEN SPACE THAT COULD BE USED BY ALL THE PEOPLE IN YOUR NEIGHBOURHOOD SHOWING HOW IT WOULD FUNCTION.

THE VILLAGE GREEN HAS PROVED TO BE FUNCTIONAL AND AS SUCH COMMUNITIES SHOULD ALL BE PROVIDED WITH A SORT OF VILLAGE GREEN FOR A LIMITED NUMBER OF [illegible] THE 'GREEN' COMMUNITY REQUIRES THE GREEN OPEN SPACE WITH TREES AND LARGE POOL FOR BOATING/PICNIC. THE WHOLE SURROUNDED BY SHOPS (LIMITED) PUBS, EATING HOUSES, AND SOCIAL CENTRES, SWIMMING POOL, LIBRARIES, EMPLOYMENT OFFICE BUT [illegible] WITHIN CLOSE TOUCH AND FRONTING THE GREEN AS MUCH AS POSSIBLE. SHOPPING CENTRES ARE CLOSE BUT NOT FRONTING THE GREEN PREFERABLY AT RIGHT ANGLES TO AND IN PARADES. ALL MOTOR TRAFFIC IS REMOVED AND [illegible] OVER OR UNDER THE SHOPS. PARKING NOT ALLOWED IN FRONT OF HOUSES – EITHER GARAGED OR AT BACK

Project area two: Osterley

f

SHEET FIVE.

DESCRIBE, DRAW, MAKE A MAP OF HOW YOU THINK YOUR HOUSE, GARDEN ETC SHOULD RELATE TO YOUR NEIGHBOURS.

DESCRIBE AND MAKE A PLAN OF A GARDEN OR OPEN SPACE THAT COULD BE USED BY ALL THE PEOPLE IN YOUR NEIGHBOURHOOD SHOWING HOW IT WOULD FUNCTION.

e

SHEET EIGHT.

HOW WOULD YOU ORGANISE PUBLIC/PRIVATE TRANSPORT FACILITIES TO MEET ON ONE HAND YOUR OWN AND ON THE OTHER GENERAL COMMUNITY NEEDS. DESCRIBE, DRAW A MAP.

GREATER. LONDON.

Car Parks on all major trunk Roads into London.

HOW WOULD YOU ORGANISE CUTURAL ACTIVITIES TO MEET ON ONE HAND YOUR OWN AND ON THE OTHER GENERAL COMMUNITY NEEDS.

A Council Run Sports & Community Center
[illegible] with grounds for football cricket and a gym
for Indoor Sport. Center to have bar and a [illegible]
fee which should be charged for Membership
A [illegible] should be put aside for the Old people
and a Space for a Playgroup

Project area two: Osterley

e

SHEET NINE

DESCRIBE, DRAW, MAKE A MAP OF THE HOUSING LAYOUT THAT YOU SEE AS SERVING YOUR OWN AND GENERAL COMMUNITY NEEDS.

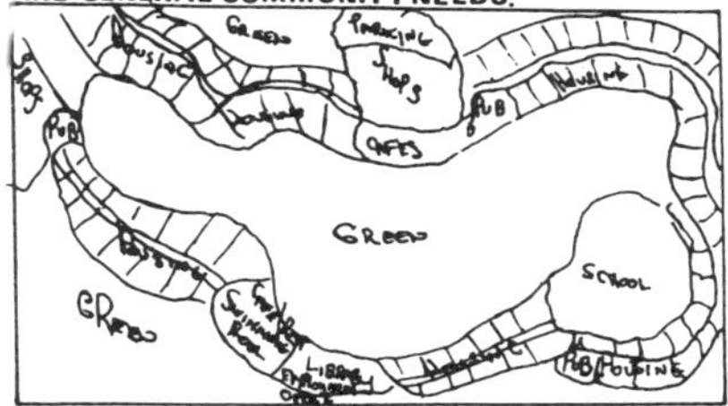

WHAT DO YOU SEE AS THE IDEAL SOCIAL STRUCTURE FOR YOUR NEIGHBOURHOOD, AND ITS RELATIONSHIP TO OTHER COMMUNITIES IN WEST LONDON.

I DO NOT SEE ANY SOCIAL STRUCTURE HAVING A RELATIONSHIP TO OTHER COMMUNITIES IN WEST LONDON. THE INDIVIDUAL COMMUNITIES WILL HAVE TO BE DEVELOPED SEPARATELY ALBEIT TO A SIMILAR PATTERN

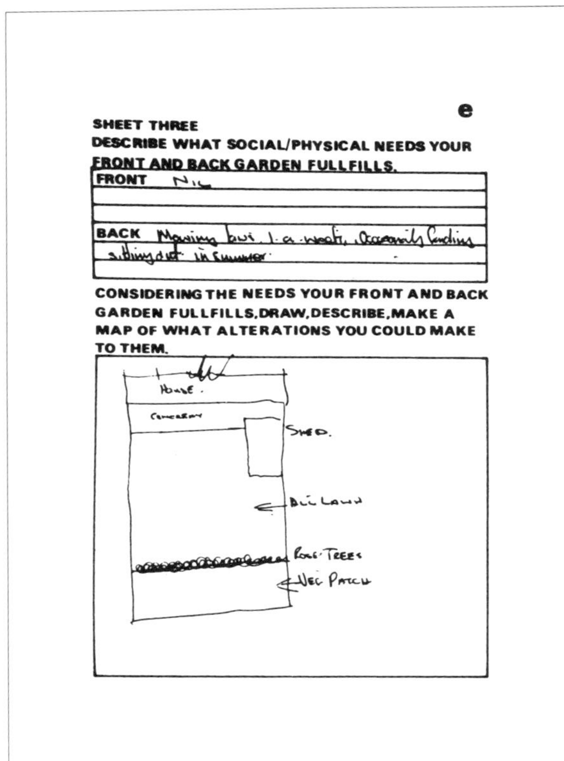

e

SHEET THREE

DESCRIBE WHAT SOCIAL/PHYSICAL NEEDS YOUR FRONT AND BACK GARDEN FULLFILLS.

FRONT Nil

BACK Mowing lawn 1 a week, Occasionally Gardening sitting out in summer

CONSIDERING THE NEEDS YOUR FRONT AND BACK GARDEN FULLFILLS, DRAW, DESCRIBE, MAKE A MAP OF WHAT ALTERATIONS YOU COULD MAKE TO THEM.

Project area three: Hanwell

k

SHEET THREE

DESCRIBE WHAT SOCIAL/PHYSICAL NEEDS YOUR FRONT AND BACK GARDEN FULLFILLS.

FRONT None other than keeping house at a distance from road.

BACK Childrens play area

CONSIDERING THE NEEDS YOUR FRONT AND BACK GARDEN FULLFILLS, DRAW, DESCRIBE, MAKE A MAP OF WHAT ALTERATIONS YOU COULD MAKE TO THEM.

Front

Drive
grass
grass
House
present plan

Drive
paved front
projected plan

A porch has just been completed with door deliberately opening outward so that it provides easier access from drive. Next year we plan to re arrange the garden as it is so fragmented at the moment. We feel the effect of an open area before the house will [illegible] the aspect.

SHEET SIX. **g**

MAKE A MAP OF YOUR NEIGHBOUGHOOD SHOWING HOW IT RELATES TO EXISTING SOCIAL FACILITIES, SUCH AS SHOPS, LIBRARIES, SCHOOLS, SPORTS CLUBS ETC.

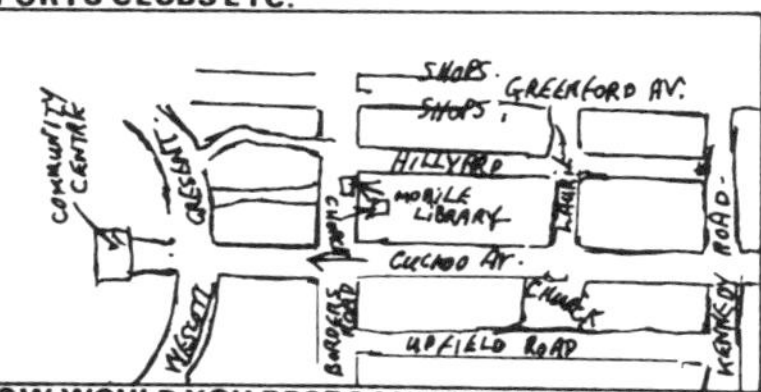

HOW WOULD YOU REORGANISE THE ABOVE MAP IN ORDER TO MAKE THE SOCIAL FACILITIES SERVE WHAT YOU CONSIDER YOUR NEIGHBOUGHOOD NEEDS TO BE. DESCRIBE AND DRAW A MAP.

WHERE THE HANWELL COMMUNITY CENTRE IS SITUATED, CHURCH AND MOBILE LIBRARY WOULD BE ALLSO IN THIS AREA. MORE HOUSES COULD BE BUILT ON VACATED SPACES INSTEAD OF THE EYESORE THEY ARE AT THE MOMENT.

Project area three: Hanwell

k

SHEET EIGHT.

HOW WOULD YOU ORGANISE PUBLIC/PRIVATE TRANSPORT FACILITIES TO MEET ON ONE HAND YOUR OWN AND ON THE OTHER GENERAL COMMUNITY NEEDS. DESCRIBE, DRAW A MAP.

The primary schoolchildren from this side of the West Road attend Heaton School which is over 1 mile from here & they must follow Jersey Rd which is a 'loop' road & consequently busy. It is a long walk for 5 yr olds & hazardous. Most children get lifts in private cars which must cause chaos at the school end as it is on a busy through route. A small scale bus service could be organised perhaps on a private basis. Otherwise satisfactory (There would be several ↗ pick up & laying down points en route)

HOW WOULD YOU ORGANISE CUTURAL ACTIVITIES TO MEET ON ONE HAND YOUR OWN AND ON THE OTHER GENERAL COMMUNITY NEEDS.

A large centre where all arts can be particip[ated] & appreciated – art, films, plays, music, sport etc on an amateur & professional level. As this cultural centre would of necessity need to be more than the size of one hall – (or a complex rather than a hall) & there is no suitable 'place' locally perhaps some arrangement can be made with one of the local colleges of further education – Romford Rd, Ilford Poly – [illegible] amount of enthusiasm & ideas if not actual space.

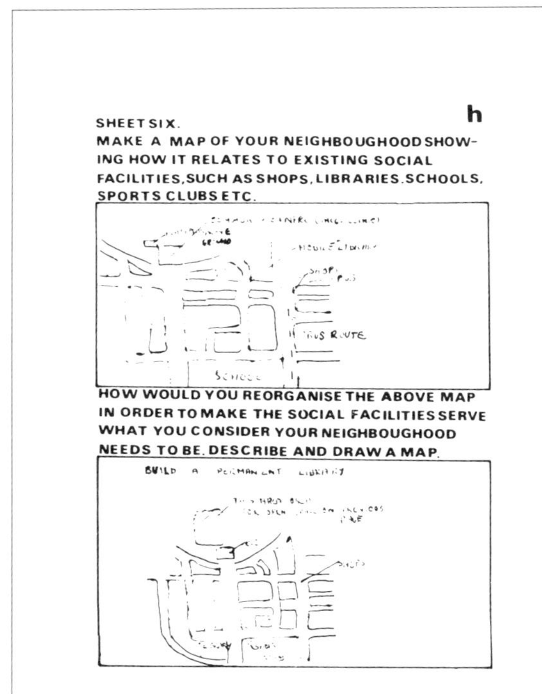

h

SHEET SIX.

MAKE A MAP OF YOUR NEIGHBOUGHOOD SHOWING HOW IT RELATES TO EXISTING SOCIAL FACILITIES, SUCH AS SHOPS, LIBRARIES, SCHOOLS, SPORTS CLUBS ETC.

HOW WOULD YOU REORGANISE THE ABOVE MAP IN ORDER TO MAKE THE SOCIAL FACILITIES SERVE WHAT YOU CONSIDER YOUR NEIGHBOUGHOOD NEEDS TO BE. DESCRIBE AND DRAW A MAP.

Project area three: Hanwell

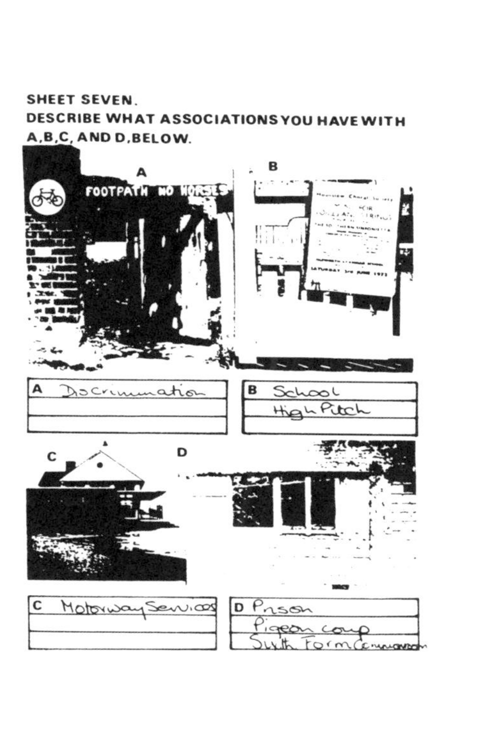

SHEET SEVEN.
DESCRIBE WHAT ASSOCIATIONS YOU HAVE WITH A,B,C, AND D,BELOW.

A Discrimination

B School
High Pitch

C Motorway Services

D Prison
Pigeon coup
Sixth Form Commonroom

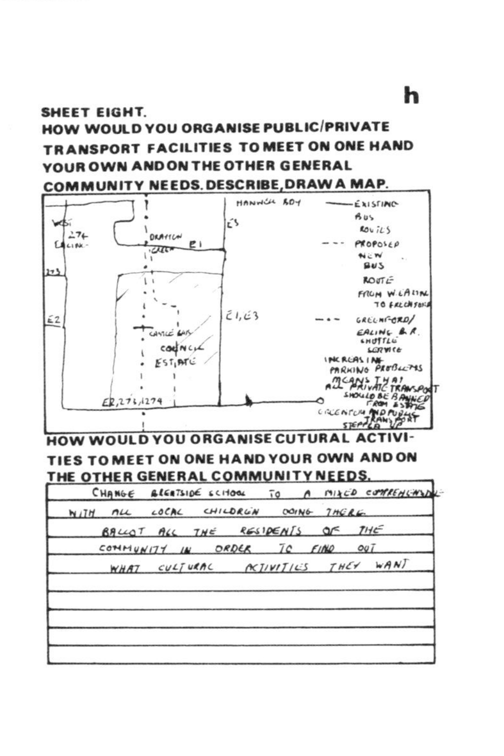

h

SHEET EIGHT.
HOW WOULD YOU ORGANISE PUBLIC/PRIVATE TRANSPORT FACILITIES TO MEET ON ONE HAND YOUR OWN AND ON THE OTHER GENERAL COMMUNITY NEEDS. DESCRIBE, DRAW A MAP.

HOW WOULD YOU ORGANISE CUTURAL ACTIVITIES TO MEET ON ONE HAND YOUR OWN AND ON THE OTHER GENERAL COMMUNITY NEEDS.

CHANGE BRENTSIDE SCHOOL TO A MIXED COMPREHENSIVE
WITH ALL LOCAL CHILDREN GOING THERE.
BALLOT ALL THE RESIDENTS OF THE
COMMUNITY IN ORDER TO FIND OUT
WHAT CULTURAL ACTIVITIES THEY WANT

Project area three: Hanwell

a

SHEET NINE

DESCRIBE, DRAW, MAKE A MAP OF THE HOUSING LAYOUT THAT YOU SEE AS SERVING YOUR OWN AND GENERAL COMMUNITY NEEDS.

More flats for the old
in fact convert the whole
Cuckoo estate to all old folk
& resident doctors with their
own clinic to cater for the estate
All authorities could house their
older citizens giving more chances
for the young to get houses

WHAT DO YOU SEE AS THE IDEAL SOCIAL STRUCTURE FOR YOUR NEIGHBOURHOOD, AND ITS RELATIONSHIP TO OTHER COMMUNITIES IN WEST LONDON.

The above ~~covers~~
covers all the
questions

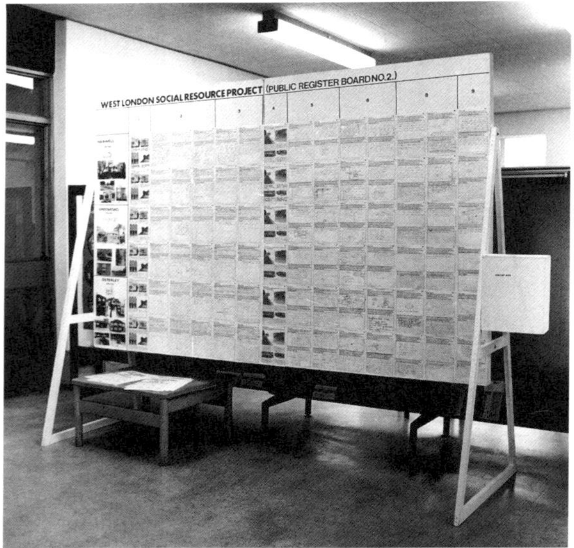

FIGURE 16 Public register board no. 2. Situated in a branch library adjacent to one of the project areas. Displayed on the board were participant returns from the West London Re-modelling Book. Participants were invited to record their preferences from the displayed returns on a public decision slip, left on a small table in front of the board. Completed decision slips were deposited in the ballot box fixed to the side of the board.

WEST LONDON SOCIAL RESOURCE PROJECT

PUBLIC DECISION SLIP

ON THE PUBLIC REGISTER BOARD PARTICIPANT RETURNS HAVE BEEN DIVIDED INTO SHEET NUMBERS. EACH RETURN UNDER A PARTICULAR SHEET NUMBER HAS BEEN GIVEN A LETTER,7A,6G ETC.
EXAMINE THE RETURNS UNDER A SHEET NUMBER,THEN SELECT THE ONE YOU CONSIDER TO BE THE MOST ORIGINAL,RELEVANT ETC. RECORD YOUR DECISION IN THE SPACE BELOW,ADDING SOME COMMENTS IN THE SPACE PROVIDED IF YOU WANT TO.
A PERSON DOES NOT HAVE TO HAVE BEEN INVOLVED IN THE COMPLETION OF THE BOOK TO FILL IN A PUBLIC DECISION SLIP.

No.1 Letter____	No.2 Letter____	No.3 Letter____	No.4 Letter____
No.5 Letter____	No.6 Letter____	No.8 Letter____	No.9 Letter____

FIGURE 17 Public decision slips were used by participants to record their preferences for returns from the re-modelling book.

PARTICIPANT RECORDS. PUBLIC DECISION SLIP RETURNS.

VOTING TOTALS.

Sheet One		Sheet Two		Sheet Three		Sheet Four		Sheet Five		S
Number	Letter	Number	Letter	Number	Letter	Number	Letter	Number	Letter	Nu
3	F	2	I	1	H	4	A	1	G	1
1	A	3	A	4	I	1	B	1	B	5
4	D	3	H	1	B	1	E	2	J	2
2	B	1	K	1	D	1	J	1	K	
1	E	1	B	1	C	1	D	2	A	
		1	Q	1	K			1	C	
		1	G					1	D	
4	D	3	H	4	I	4	A	2	J	5
		3	A					2	A	

FIGURE 18 This table shows the number of votes cast for the participant returns reproduced in figure 17. For example, sheet one, from the re-modelling book shows that example D received four votes, as shown in the bottom row.

	Sheet Eight		Sheet Nine	
r	Number	Letter	Number	Letter
	3	D	5	F
	1	K	2	D
	1	F	1	J
	1	B	1	B
	1	E	1	G
	1	C		
	1	I		
	3	D	5	F

FIGURE 19 The following pages show the final project models. These were derived from a straight count of the preferences shown in the public decision slips. These preferences were reproduced in a booklet which was distributed to participants so that they could make comparisons between their own models, recorded in their retained copies of the manual and re-modelling book, and the consensus view. The project area that returns are derived from is shown by the letters PA1, etc.

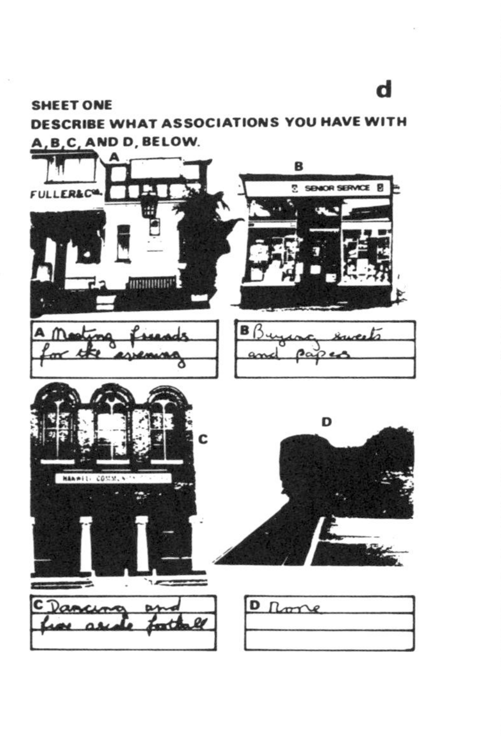
d
SHEET ONE
DESCRIBE WHAT ASSOCIATIONS YOU HAVE WITH
A, B, C, AND D, BELOW.
A
FULLER&Co.
B
SENIOR SERVICE
A Meeting friends for the evening
B Buying sweets and papers
C
D
C Dancing and five aside football
D None

p

SHEET TWO

DESCRIBE WHAT SOCIAL/PHYSICAL NEEDS THE HOUSE YOU LIVE IN FULLFILLS.

The house I live in is close to all shops and many bus routes so it is easy to visit places of entertainment and to visit friends and also for our friends to visit us.

The kitchen is too small for comfort.

DESCRIBE, DRAW, MAKE A MAP OF WHAT CHANGES IF ANY COULD BE MADE TO THE INTERIOR OF THE HOUSE YOU LIVE IN, SHOWING HOW THEY RELATE TO THE NEEDS IT FULLFILLS.

a

SHEET TWO

DESCRIBE WHAT SOCIAL/PHYSICAL NEEDS THE HOUSE YOU LIVE IN FULLFILLS.

THE NEED FOR EVERY ONE IN THE FAMILY TO GET TOGETHER, EAT DRINK AND REST AND RELAX IN ONES OWN LITTLE PASSTIMES. AND TO ENTERTAIN ONES FRIENDS.

DESCRIBE, DRAW, MAKE A MAP OF WHAT CHANGES IF ANY COULD BE MADE TO THE INTERIOR OF THE HOUSE YOU LIVE IN, SHOWING HOW THEY RELATE TO THE NEEDS IT FULLFILLS.

WE WOULD LIKE MORE SPACE IN GROUND FLOOR ROOMS, EXTEND FRONT ROOM INTO KITCHEN, HAVE EXTENSION ON BACK OF HOUSE, THIS WOULD MAKE DECORATING AND CLEANING EASIER, STOP A CERTAIN AMOUNT OF DRAUGHT, BUILT IN BAY WINDOW AND FRONT PORCH WOULD GIVE THE HOUSE MORE CARACTER. NO MORE FURNITURE WOULD BE NEEDED. THE EXTENSION BEING HANDY FOR A PLAY ROOM FOR CHILDREN

i

SHEET THREE

DESCRIBE WHAT SOCIAL/PHYSICAL NEEDS YOUR FRONT AND BACK GARDEN FULLFILLS.

FRONT	A PLACE TO PARK MY BIKE
BACK	A PLACE TO PARK MYSELF

CONSIDERING THE NEEDS YOUR FRONT AND BACK GARDEN FULLFILLS, DRAW, DESCRIBE, MAKE A MAP OF WHAT ALTERATIONS YOU COULD MAKE TO THEM.

ELIZABETH TAYLOR'S SWIMMING POOL

COMPLETE WITH ELIZABETH TAYLOR

a

SHEET FIVE.

DESCRIBE, DRAW, MAKE A MAP OF HOW YOU THINK YOUR HOUSE, GARDEN ETC SHOULD RELATE TO YOUR NEIGHBOURS.

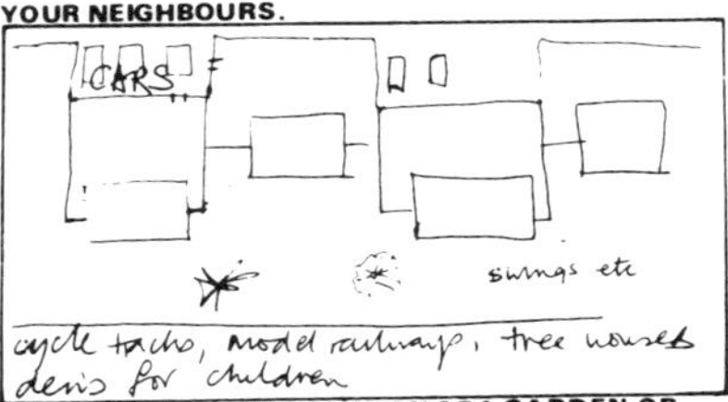

DESCRIBE AND MAKE A PLAN OF A GARDEN OR OPEN SPACE THAT COULD BE USED BY ALL THE PEOPLE IN YOUR NEIGHBOURHOOD SHOWING HOW IT WOULD FUNCTION.

the communal garden as described above can be used by children, parents and visitors, the houses being situated so that a mother can see the children playing easily

C

SHEET SIX.

MAKE A MAP OF YOUR NEIGHBOUGHOOD SHOWING HOW IT RELATES TO EXISTING SOCIAL FACILITIES, SUCH AS SHOPS, LIBRARIES, SCHOOLS, SPORTS CLUBS ETC.

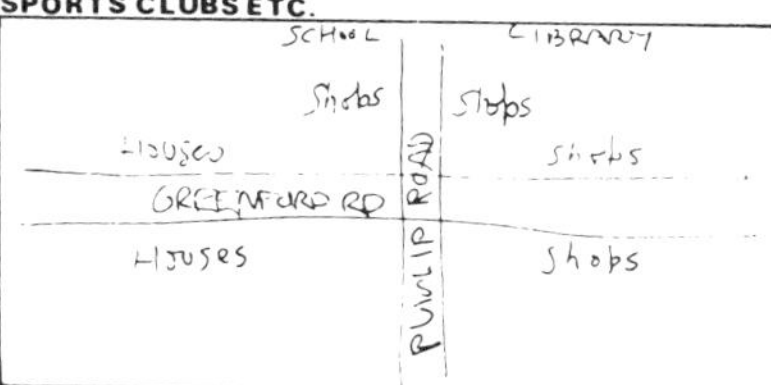

HOW WOULD YOU REORGANISE THE ABOVE MAP IN ORDER TO MAKE THE SOCIAL FACILITIES SERVE WHAT YOU CONSIDER YOUR NEIGHBOUGHOOD NEEDS TO BE. DESCRIBE AND DRAW A MAP.

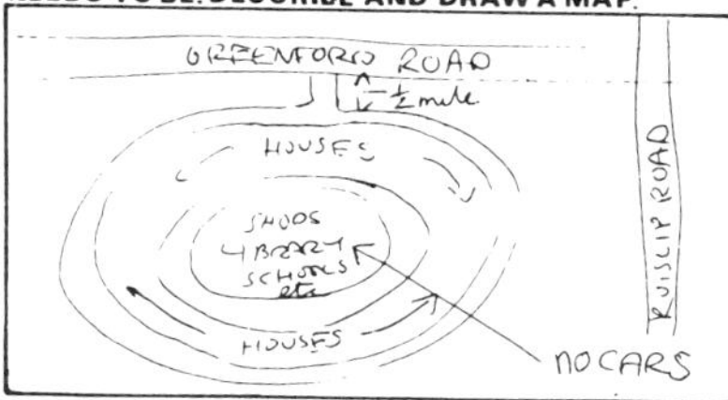

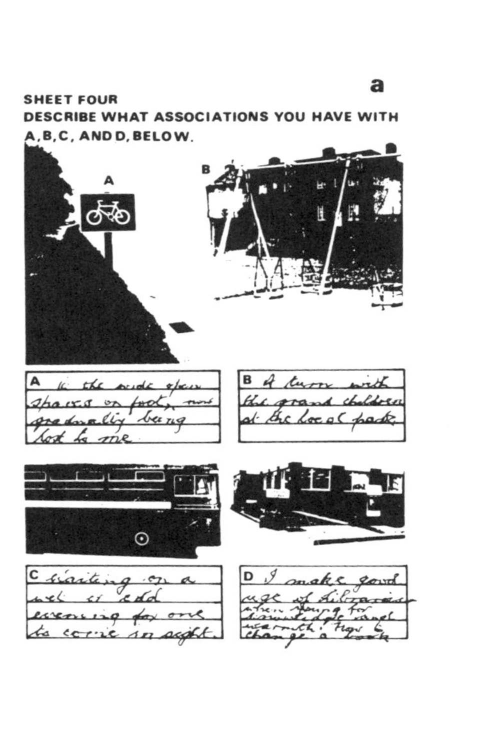
a
SHEET FOUR
DESCRIBE WHAT ASSOCIATIONS YOU HAVE WITH
A, B, C, AND D, BELOW.
A
B
A ... the wide open spaces on foot, now gradually being lost to me
B A turn with the grand children at the local park.
C waiting on a wet or cold evening for one to come in sight.
D I make good use of libraries

j

SHEET FIVE.

DESCRIBE, DRAW, MAKE A MAP OF HOW YOU THINK YOUR HOUSE, GARDEN ETC SHOULD RELATE TO YOUR NEIGHBOURS.

ALL HOUSES TO BE DETACHED

None of this back to front as most houses are at present

DESCRIBE AND MAKE A PLAN OF A GARDEN OR OPEN SPACE THAT COULD BE USED BY ALL THE PEOPLE IN YOUR NEIGHBOURHOOD SHOWING HOW IT WOULD FUNCTION.

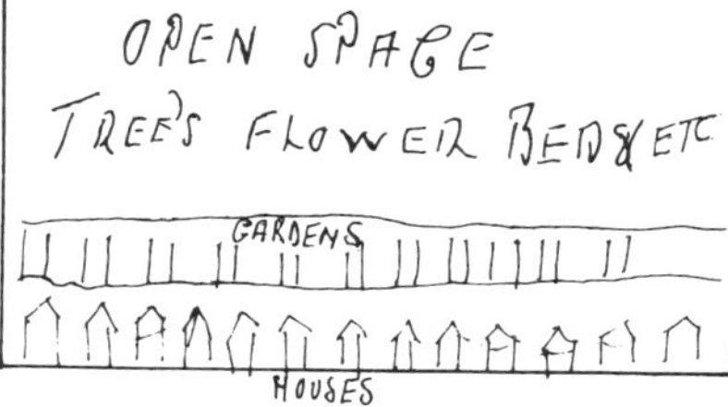

d

SHEET EIGHT.

HOW WOULD YOU ORGANISE PUBLIC/PRIVATE TRANSPORT FACILITIES TO MEET ON ONE HAND YOUR OWN AND ON THE OTHER GENERAL COMMUNITY NEEDS. DESCRIBE, DRAW A MAP.

PEOPLE SHOULD NOT BE ALLOWED TO TRAVEL TO TOWN WITH LARGE CARS AND CARRY ONE PASSENGER (THEMSELVES) BY DOING THIS [THE DRIVER] IT MAKES ABOUT FOUR TIMES AS MANY VEHICLES ON THE ROAD. ALSO LARGE LORRIES ETC SHOULD NOT BE ALLOWED ON ROADS AT ALL USE THE RAILWAYS AND MAKE THEM PAY. ALSO ON THE BUSES SUGGEST SOMETHING SHOULD BE DONE THAT DOESN'T SLIP. LEATHER STRAPS?

HOW WOULD YOU ORGANISE CUTURAL ACTIVITIES TO MEET ON ONE HAND YOUR OWN AND ON THE OTHER GENERAL COMMUNITY NEEDS.

I WOULD OPEN THE CINEMAS AGAIN - THEY KEEP YOUNG FOLK OFF THE STREETS AT NIGHT AND CHILDREN OCCUPIED ON SATURDAY MORNING. BRING THE PRICES DOWN SUBSIDISE THEM IF NECESSARY. THE COST TO THE COUNCIL WOULD BE CHEAPER THAN HAVING TO REPAIR DAMAGE DONE BY BORED YOUNG VANDALS. ALSO PLEASE A BAND IN THE PARK ON SUNDAYS

SHEET NINE **f**

DESCRIBE, DRAW, MAKE A MAP OF THE HOUSING LAYOUT THAT YOU SEE AS SERVING YOUR OWN AND GENERAL COMMUNITY NEEDS.

Parks Nearby
A Rest Garden for the Old
Libraries Nearby
Meals-on-Wheels & Home
Helps for the old &
bedridden

WHAT DO YOU SEE AS THE IDEAL SOCIAL STRUCTURE FOR YOUR NEIGHBOURHOOD, AND ITS RELATIONSHIP TO OTHER COMMUNITIES IN WEST LONDON.

House types should be mixed so as to provide for and encourage a cross-section of population (ages income groups family structures) in each local community. Groups of streets and even individual streets should contain such a mixture of houses. This might improve communication between generations & break down class barriers. It might also make streets architecturally less boring

the edinburgh social model construction project

theoretical model

The central feature of the West London Project and other earlier projects was the process with which they enabled models to be constructed by an individual in relation to those generated by the social group (participant group) to which he belonged. This process was the conceptualisation from which the rest of the project was structured. The conceptual form of the model-constructing process in the Edinburgh project resulted in a different structure from the other projects. The Edinburgh project concerned a different area of a participant's world: instead of involving the coding of the physical structure of a person's immediate environment, it centred on the coding of interpersonal behaviour. Earlier projects had required people to make links from their physical environment, to their behaviour within it. The Edinburgh Social Model Construction Project took a person's behaviour in relation to other people as a starting point, but it did so in relation to the environment in which that behaviour existed.

The project's area of attention involved people's perception of the coding of interpersonal behaviour which had become a convention or an established routine within the different social groups. The reason for centring the project's concerns on interpersonal coding was because we considered that the foundation of social behaviour was largely derived from the coding conventions that had been acquired by the individual, or had been reinforced by the community to which he belonged. In structuring interpersonal relationships, 'life codes' have an important role in establishing relative positions between people, especially at the level of casual contact, and were thus included within the project's concerns. The acquisition of interpersonal coding conventions by an individual was seen to be a basis for his subsequent social interactions, and a participant could thus relate them, we thought, to diverse social contexts. By increasing a participant's awareness of his own coding behaviour, he would become able to contextualise the project's concerns by relating, or integrating, the different situations with which he was presented to his own experience.

The model-constructing process embodied in the project was designed to facilitate the re-modelling by participants of their own coding structures. At the same time it presented participants with a model of a 'life code'. This model was constructed around the concept of homeostasis (see figure 20). The homeostatic model was intended to exemplify the concepts generated in cybernetics of self-organising systems (see figure 21). The homeostatic model was envisaged as forming the framework of the project. It consisted of a mechanism which would function over a theoretically infinite period of time, during the course of which it would generate sequences of interdependent models.[25] In its abstract state the homeostat consisted of four interconnected nodes (project areas), which in themselves were comprised of subnodes (participants), which were linked together through a processing node, called the central core, the operational centre of the project (see figure 22).

As a theoretical mechanism it was given the practical environment of Edinburgh and it was formulated with the inbuilt specification of seeking an equilibrium within its own structure. This state was considered achieved when the four interconnected nodes had attained a common information level. The environment was to be comprised of potential problems and was thus called the 'problem environment'.[26] In order to find stability, the homeostat would need to have solved any problems it encountered within the problem environment. Any change of state in the problem environment would upset stability and thus generate a new category of problems. As the project's area of attention concerned different aspects of interpersonal behaviour conventions, the problems were centred on this aspect of the homeostat's environment. The solutions to problems were in the form of models constructed by sub-nodes (participants): these were then to be formed into a consensus for each node (project area). The communication of models from node to node was the means by which equilibrium was to be achieved. As changes in the problem environment took place, so the homeostat was to develop solutions to the problems generated, and as a consequence evolve its own hierarchy of models. Changes within the problem environment were to be sequentially linked. Solutions to one set of problems could then form a heuristic to the provision of solutions to subsequent ones (see figure 23). Heuristics were intended to combine to form more powerful ones, which could be applied to future changes of state in the problem environment.[27]

The models constructed by sub-nodes in response to problems were to consist of those from the three categories – descriptive, predictive, prescriptive – that have already been outlined. As the hierarchy of models was constructed they were to be gradually directed towards priorities expressed in previously formed models created by each node. This effectively meant that as the project progressed each node's models would develop their own direction, but the interconnections in the homeostat would enable these separate pursuits to come together to form a coherent integrated whole, representing four different viewpoints at any one time. The self direction of models was not to be totally free, as it depended on how each node viewed the categories of interpersonal behaviour linked to changes of state in the problem environment. The two functions – arriving at equilibrium within each node, and deriving new problems from it – were to be undertaken within the central core. The central core and nodes were connected by an information channel which retrieved the models created by sub-nodes and fed them into the central core for processing. After a short delay the consensus viewpoint, i.e. a new baseline, was communicated to each of the nodes, while at the same time they were represented with new sets of problems. The consensus viewpoint was extracted from a node's retrieved models by the central core, and formalised into a short statement on which to base the orientation of new problems, and to communicate with the other nodes. This procedure was to be undertaken separately for each of the nodes. As a theoretical model the process of interaction between nodes and the central core would result in constant change.

the practical model

The theoretical model provided the conception for a more practical one, which was associated with implementing the project as an operational entity.[28] While the theoretical model provided the structural essence of the project, the practical one provided the detail necessary to carry it out. Before a methodology was arrived at, a number of decisions had to be made about the context it was to operate within, and the nature of the audience.[29] These considerations were similar to those made when formulating the West London Project, as both audience composition and location were similar. As a result of these considerations, the audience's existing routines within their residential neighbourhoods were specified as suitable contexts for the project to operate in. Each of the participant groups was envisaged as representing a social group distinctly different and physically separate from the others. It was thought that the difference between the four groups would be a contributory factor in creating distinct viewpoints of the project's concerns.

The methodologies employed in the project were intended to be essentially task-oriented, participants being given a series of tasks to complete by the central core. These tasks were in the form of problems that were open in their construction, and ambiguously phrased as questions. The tasks were of two kinds. The first kind of tasks were called 'monitoring assignments', and these required a participant to construct descriptive models of his own and other people's interpersonal coding structures. The second kind were called 'problems', and involved a participant in constructing prescriptive models as solutions. Problems were in turn split into two basic types: those which concerned a participant's own social group (a sub-node's relationship to other sub-nodes within the same node), and those which concerned a participant's relationship to other sub-nodes within other nodes. Two problems divided in this fashion always followed a monitoring assignment, having the same area of attention. So if a monitoring assignment concerned a participant's perception of family meal time, so would the two accompanying problems (see figure 24). Project states were structured into a sequence of 'problem categories', which acted as basic elements in a learning system that formalised the interactive process between the central core and nodes in the theoretical model (see figure 25).

As pointed out, the number of state changes in the problem environment was potentially infinite; however, only a small number could be considered in this project. Five problem categories were arrived at, as the ideal number that would cover a wide range of behaviour conventions without overlapping too much, ranging from problems concerning a participant's immediate family environment to those of wider society. A full description of the problem categories and their related contexts is given in figure 25.

The role of problem categories in the project was to determine the orientation of problems for each individual project state, without giving their actual composition, this latter decision being arrived at through processing carried out in the central core. Integral to the processing were 12 prespecified problem sub-categories which were intended to give variety to each problem category. Problem sub-categories were split into two fundamental types in much the same way as problems; the first concerned a participant's intimate models of his own social group, and the second involved distance models of other social groups. The two kinds of problem sub-category formed a sequence from 1 to 12 (see figure 25), starting with 'an individual's perception of x'; together with 'other individuals' perception of x', and ending with 'different social groups' perception of x'. x, as seen in the diagram, refers to the problem category relating to whichever project state is in operation.

The matrix reproduced in figure 25 was used in the selection of fresh problems for each project state, each square being connected to a list of already written 'problems', and 'monitoring assignments'. From this list new tasks were to be selected. This selection was achieved by matching the priorities expressed in the consensus tendencies derived from a participant group's solutions against, firstly, the problem category of the new project state, and, secondly, the list of problem sub-categories. The consensus tendencies for each participant group's solutions were formalised into a short statement (typical examples are shown in figure 26) by a committee, who extracted that part of their contents which related to the project's concerns. The results were matched in order of expressed priority against the problem sub-categories listed in the matrix. If, for example, 60 per cent of the responses from a participant group were biased towards X, and 40 per cent to Y, then X would be used to select proportionately the majority of the next project state's problems. If it was concluded, for instance, that X represented a strong identification with neighbourhood behaviour patterns, then this would be matched against problem sub-category 5, which given the next problem category in operation, say D, would equal 5D. The problem sub-categories that achieved the best match with the consensus tendency statements in turn indicated which problems were to be selected for use from a file of already written problems. Having used the matrix to indicate the type of new problems relevant to a participant group's solutions the committee then looked at each problem in turn. Considering what aspect of 5D, for example, it was concerned with, and on the basis of a majority verdict, members selected new problems. These new problems were then delivered to participants, together with a copy of the consensus tendency statements, so that they could use them as rules of thumb in constructing fresh solutions.

Apart from the consensus tendency statements, the actual models participants had constructed were displayed on public monitor boards in their own neighbourhoods. The public monitor boards were structured so that they formed a file which showed each of the participant group's responses to an individual project state. Models displayed on the public monitors were intended for use by a participant in conjunction with the consensus tendency statements to provide a basis of information for the development of new solutions. While the consensus provided participants with a general indication of tendencies or priorities that had been expressed in models, the public monitors were to provide the opportunity for a more detailed examination. In addition the public monitors enabled personal comparisons to be made between project states, participant groups, and individual returns.

the operation of the project

This description of the operation of the Social Model Construction Project concerns the events that took place in setting it up in the field and the logistical problems of undertaking it on a daily basis. Inevitably, the practicalities of carrying out such a project meant that the original theoretical model, while it might serve as a basis for formulating the activities necessary to its implementation, required a different form of discussion. The possibility of unforeseen events meant that there could be a great deal of difference between the theory and practice of a project such as the Social Model Construction Project. While these certainly did occur in this case, the original conception was, with a few small deviations, completely realised. As previously explained I was invited early in 1973 to plan a project that would take place during the Leith and Edinburgh Festivals at the end of August that year. Work was started on planning the project in March, and with the help of Luijana Miklasz, a number of reconnaissance trips were made around this time to select suitable locations for the project. Each location (project area) had to be a residential neighbourhood, whose inhabitants generally identified themselves with a distinct social group. Project areas were selected within the following districts of Edinburgh: project area one, Leith; project area two, Morningside; project area three, Slateford; project area four, Silverknowes (see figure 27). A project area consisted of a few interconnected streets in the aforementioned districts, which were a few miles apart (see figure 28).

After the project areas had been selected and photographically documented, work started on designing the detail of project strategies. While this work was going on, a team of project operators were gathered together and grouped into three supervisory teams which were allocated specific functions in maintaining the daily operations of the project. Before the start of the project a meeting was called in Edinburgh with all the project operators present, to discuss which supervisory team they would like to join, and to describe in detail what their functions were. They were then given a copy of the project operators' manual, which gave instructions as to how they should carry out the running of the project. One of the supervisory teams was allocated the role of initiating and maintaining the project in the project areas, a second was concerned with running the central core, and the third with organising the display of models on the public monitors.

The project lasted for five days, between Monday 27 August and Friday 31 August, one day in this period equalling one project state. The team that worked in the project areas was called the project area supervisory team. This team had the largest number of project operators, which were divided into four groups, one for each project area. At the start of the project these four teams had the task of gathering participants from the project areas two days before the project got under way. Participants were gathered by introducing the project to residents on their doorsteps, explaining in full its objectives and what was entailed in taking part. The introductory meeting was much the same as that in the West London Project, and if a person agreed to take part he was given a window poster and project file. The window poster concept had been rethought for this project, though the intended effect was the same, and one was specially designed for each project area (see figure 29). The project file was a simple folder, with brief details describing the project, and instructions for participants printed on its inside cover. The project file was provided for a participant to keep a complete record of his responses, which would gradually build up into a body of stored information, as the project progressed through its various project states.

As in earlier projects, one in every two people asked to participate agreed to take part, irrespective of the project area. The average number of participants gathered for each project area was 32. Having obtained their complement of participants the various project area supervisory teams were ready to initiate the first project state in their respective project areas. Participants were given their first set of problems in the early evening of the first day of the project by a member of their project area supervisory team. The solutions were collected before 10.00 the following morning. This procedure was followed throughout the project. The tasks (monitoring assignments) and problems that participants were given to complete, together with the consensus tendency statements, were all presented on problem sheets (figure 30). The sheets (A4 size) that contained the monitoring assignments also had a space for reproducing the consensus tendency statements. They were always presented to participants in duplicate with a sheet of carbon paper provided to enable a copy to be made of all entries. The top copy was collected by the project area supervisory team, and participants retained the carbon copy, which they stored in the project file. The collected problem sheets were then taken to a room in the university computing centre. This room housed the central core, and here another team of project operators called the central core supervisory team had the task of processing the returns, constructing the consensus tendency statements, and selecting new problems (see figure 31).

Four committees were established, one for each project area. A procedure was set up for each team for examining their project area's returns. Each member studied the contents entered on a project sheet and wrote down what he considered to be the essential meaning in a short statement. So if there were six members in one of the teams, there would be six opinions on what the contents represented. After all of a project area's returns had been examined, the six members compared their notes for each individual return, and correlated them. From this activity six sets of notes were reduced to one list, which was then used to derive the consensus tendencies, repeating much the same process. On average each team would process about 100 project sheets, made up of approximately 60 monitoring assignments and 120 problems. The result of this activity was a series of averages which were ordered into a hierarchy according to the priorities expressed. If none of the problems listed in the file were considered suitable for the consensus tendency statement, then they could be altered, or new ones written, though this only occurred once during the project. This process was repeated by each of the four teams, so that by early afternoon four sets of new problems were chosen and circulated to participants. This sequence of events took place until all five project states were completed.

Another important function is the cycle of events occurring after the project sheets had been processed by the four teams, when they were collected for display by the public monitor board supervisory team. Public monitors were housed in a golf club and a community centre, which acted as a resource for residents of project areas and surrounding districts. When visiting the boards, participants could, by taking their project file with their stored responses, make their own comparisons between the displayed returns (see figure 32).

The intended effect of this activity was much the same as the West London Project, though the creation of a secondary audience was now anticipated and indeed seen as an important feature of the project's communicative performance. In fact the secondary audience involved a larger number of people than the total of participants, though if one takes into account all the different degrees of secondary involvement (i.e. a person might get to hear about the project through a friend but not see a public monitor, or only see one by chance), it is impossible to estimate its size. As there was no publicity other than provided in the project's strategies, the secondary audience was created through neighbourhood response, as in other projects. The number of participants fell sharply by 50 per cent during the first project state, but thereafter there was very little decline. In fact participants who continued past the first project state became increasingly involved in its concerns, developing friendly relationships with project operators, to the extent that one had an evening meal cooked for him every evening when he called at project area two to distribute new problem sheets. Several other project operators also established close relationships with participants and had regular conversations with them.

These supervisory teams took considerable trouble to make sure that the project was as effective as possible in their particular project areas. In project area three, Slateford, the team organised its own circular letting people know they would be calling to invite them to participate and also about various other activities of the project. Similarly in project areas one and four, the teams obtained permission to use the sites they knew from personal experience would be effective places for the public monitors to be housed. In response to the participants' requests, after the project had finished in project area three, the team organised a larger poster with reproduced returns on it for people to hang in their homes. This shows a marked contrast to the response of project area four, Harrow, in the West London Project, a similar neighbourhood.

evaluation

Perhaps more than in previous projects the Edinburgh Social Model Construction Project was seen as demonstrating the notion of an optimum model as a work of art, which would adapt and respond with the following variables: audience composition and environmental context. The model's inbuilt flexibility was seen as enabling successful transfer to other contexts, provided that certain conditions were met. While the transference of the work to another location has not been tried, from the experience gained in Edinburgh there seems no reason why it should not be achieved successfully, with minor modifications. The conditions for transferring the project are listed in the project operators' manual (see figure 33). As participants' models derived from the physical and social context the project functioned within, any external evaluation of expressed meanings would be, to say the least, tentative. However, broad evaluations of the effect of the project on participants can be made by comparing participants' models with each other over the duration of the project. When this is done a broad tendency appears, confirming that the employment of previous models in the construction of new ones had a marked effect, because models became less personalised in their content and altered their references to include other perceptions, and behaviour.

The amount of creative conceptualisation can also be seen to have developed during the project, as models produced in response to 'problems' became less concerned with existing states, and more with hypothetical ones. In this sense there is the same movement registered in other projects: from descriptive to prescriptive, from the particular to the general. Another way in which this movement can be used is that initially participants constructed their models using themselves as a norm, but as the project developed they tended to acknowledge the intended direction of the project, and took into account other people's perceptions, behaviour, etc. There was an unexplained tendency towards written statements rather than drawings or maps in the way people expressed their models, which was unexpected as with earlier projects a predominantly visual response had been obtained. No research was undertaken on the effect of the project on participants for the same reasons given in the West London Project, and any information coming from participants was gleaned by project operators from their conversations with them. While accepting the possible unreliability of this information, it seems that the observations made previously about the cumulative effect of the project are borne out, and that as it developed the momentum of participants' involvement increased, in a large number of cases. In fact some of the participants wanted the project to continue, when it terminated at project state five. A reason for this of course might be that the project had no set terminating event which could symbolically be used by participants as a point of reference for attainment. This was purposefully left out in the conception of the project, as the project was intended theoretically to be seen as a stable feature of the environment of participants. However, there was a certain demand from participants for a terminating event, if only for the reason that they saw this as an end point, after which they could relinquish their involvement.

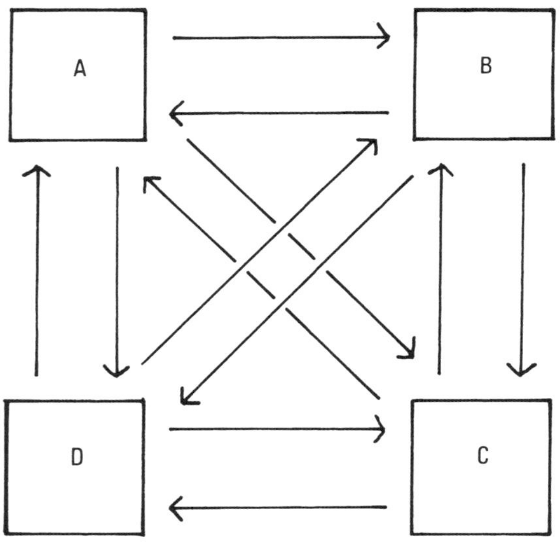

FIGURE 20 A basic model of a homeostat showing total coupling between elements A, B, C, D, thus enabling a free flow of information between any points in the structure. The system has a fundamental drive towards seeking equilibrium both within its own structure, and between itself and its environment. In this position all elements in the system have the same value.

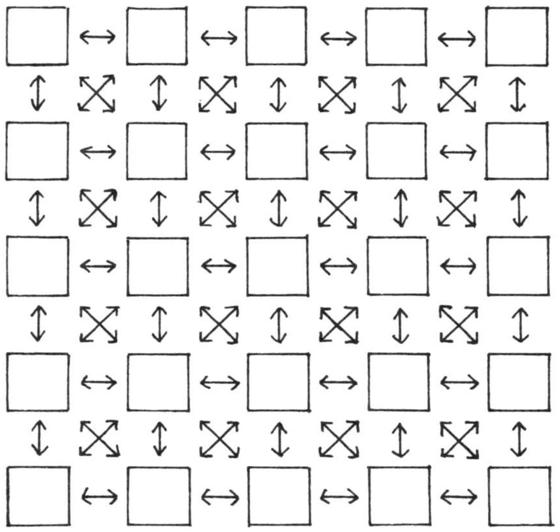

FIGURE 21 All nodes have a zero baseline. If one node obtains a plus potential the total input/output linkage means all other nodes obtain a plus potential. Thus the baseline rises, finding a new zero.

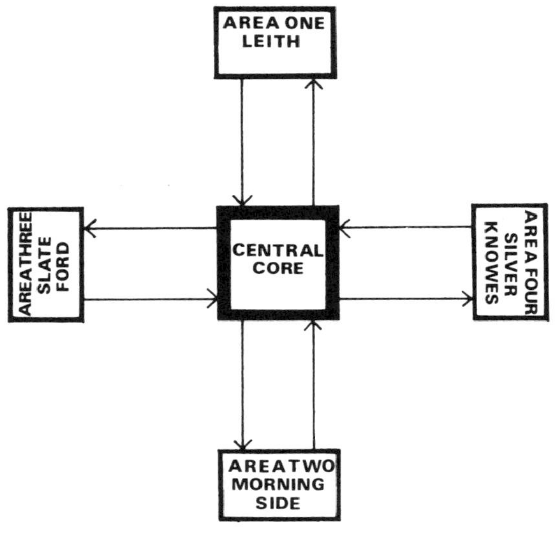

FIGURE 22 The basic structure of the work as a social model constructed around cybernetic concepts of self-organising systems.

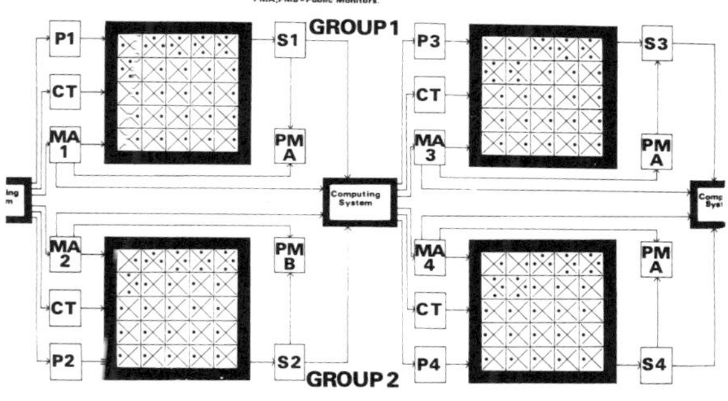

FIGURE 23 A diagrammatic representation of the relationship of participant groups and project states to each other. The diagram should be studied from left to right.

PROJECT AREA FOUR

Project state one
Problem sheet no. 1

Monitoring assignment A	'Describe how you could change your family mealtimes to meet your social needs.'
Monitoring assignment B	'Describe a typical mealtime with your family.'

Problem sheet no. 2

Problem A	'Describe/draw/make a plan of the ideal place which would be suitable for all the members of your family to go on holiday together to.'

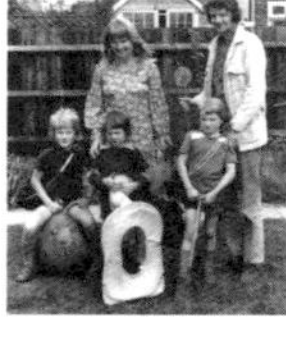

Box A

'Describe what you would imagine would be the individiual and collective activities of the members of the famly group illustrated in Box A on their annual holiday.'

Problem sheet no. 3

Problem A	'Describe how you could change your family mealtimes to meet your social needs.'
Problem B	'Draw/make a plan of how you think a typical family would position themselves around a table at Sunday lunch. Please write down their relationship to each other.'

FIGURE 24 Relationship of problems to monitoring assignments. Examples taken from project area four's problem sheets.

	PROBLEM SUB-CATERGORIES	A Behaviour conventions that govern social behaviour within the family group.	B Behaviour conventions that govern social behaviour within a social, physical neighbourhood.	C Behaviour conventions that govern social behaviour within social resources.	D Behaviour conventions that govern social behaviour within peoples jobs or profession.	E Behaviour conventions that govern social behaviour within a social group.	
							PROBLEM CATERGORIES
1	An individual participants relationship to X.	1A	1B	1C	1D	1E	1
2	Individuals from different social contexts relationship to X.	2A	2B	2C	2D	2E	2
3	A participants family's relationship to X.	3A	3B	3C	3D	3E	3
4	Families from different social contexts relationship to X.	4A	4B	4C	4D	4E	4
5	A participants social, physical neighbourhoods relationship to X.	5A	5B	5C	5D	5E	5
6	Different social, physical neighbourhoods relationship to X.	6A	6B	6C	6D	6E	6
7	Social resources used by a participant relationship to X.	7A	7B	7C	7D	7E	7
8	Social resources used by people from different social contexts relationship to X.	8A	8B	8C	8D	8E	8
9	A participant's job or professions relationship to X.	9A	9B	9C	9D	9E	9
10	People from different social contexts job or profession's relationship to X.	10A	10B	10C	10D	10E	10
11	A participant's social group's relationship to X.	11A	11B	11C	11D	11E	11
12	Different social groups relationship to X.	12A	12B	12C	12D	12E	12
		A	B	C	D	E	

FIGURE 25 Matrix used in the selection of new problem areas. A problem area was arrived at by matching a project state's problem category against the problem sub-category nearest the priorities expressed in participant returns.

PROJECT STATE ONE

Project Area One Mealtimes performed a formal social communicative role with a set seating arrangement. The jobs in the area were seen as predominantly trades and services. Staggered starting times for jobs led to little interaction between family members in the morning, but led to co-operation in a tight schedule.

Project Area Two There seems to be no set pattern for mealtimes. People were able to relate to the telephone photo, but not to the other signs shown. Family activity determined by family size. A strong feeling of property shown by the returns.

Project Area Three Limited social contact in the neighbourhood, but general social concern over neighbourhood problems. Preference for formal mealtimes and for outdoor activities outside of Edinburgh. Club shown in photo did not appeal but was thought to be concerned with sporting activities. General dislike of bingo; people would seem to prefer to fish from the pier.

Project Area Four Most families consider annual holidays essential. They prefer to spend them on their own. The ideal holiday is on a quiet beach with a small town nearby. Baby-sitters are required. Most families have a formal mealtime. Most households are family conscious and meals are seen as get-togethers.

PROJECT STATE TWO

Project Area One Jobs vary. Most people find them satisfying. Some feeling of separateness from Edinburgh. Job relationships better than neighbourhood ones. Ideally, good housing (no flats), community facilities, close but separate work places, various social backgrounds and much social interaction but doubted this would work as in Leith.

Project Area Two Picture interpreted as student greeting older woman with formal respect. Greetings defined as formal social custom, clarifying relationships. Residents see area as middle class,

FIGURE 26 Consensus tendency statements

professional and distinct from rest of Edinburgh. Charity events thought ideal for mixing all ages, classes. Ideally, area should have houses, gardens, open spaces, and trees bounded by main roads and social amenities, the latter to mix all ages.

Project Area Three Shops adequate, general amenities poor, too much bingo. No family social events. Everyone agreed on more cinemas, libraries, open spaces, gardens, seats for old people, playgrounds. Galas, sports events thought best means of mixing families from all areas. Some thought ideal neighbourhood impossible.

Project Area Four Residents associate Leith with shops, work; Morningside with social life; Murrayfield with sport; Liberton & Duddingston with friends; Slateford had no association. Most wrote church and gala events as main family social events, but competitions were considered more important than co-operative activities for promoting community spirit. From the photographs, most described leisure activities in Silverknowes as sun-bathing, gardening, car washing.

PROJECT STATE THREE

Project Area One Shops, cinemas and restaurants were used outside the area. Church activities and outdoor trips took people outside the area. Present social facilities at work were: canteen, annual dance, sports clubs. Facilities wanted: club for more contact and recreational activities. Typical activities in Area 1, social-business, recreational. Area 2, social and leisure for older people.

Project Area Two Main amenities used are sports clubs. Most memorable events were concerned with social embarrassments or obtaining prominence. Club members' ideal evening was an informal dinner and drinks – for the golf club a formal dinner dance. Social customs were seen as traditional social interaction. A boat would be used by a young middle-class family.

Project Area Three Only canteen and sports club within area. Shops, cinemas, restaurants, playgrounds used outside area, also visiting friends or taking children to playground. The boat is either a house-substitute or amusement for rich. Drinking a common element in most answers. Solution B answers very varied.
Project Area Four Church dinner dance, main social neighbourhood activity outside area, also thought the ideal evening for own club. Drinking and conversation important. Social resources used outside area mainly cinema, shops, restaurants. Attainment in sport of unexpected or interesting evenings most memorable club activities. Other areas varied by mainly bingo, sports and some social concern clubs.

PROJECT STATE FOUR
Project Area One Most people were happy with their working environment apart from schools. Working environments should be more colourful and spacious. This would lead for the most part to cheerful, more relaxed working relationships. Most families would like to run a well-organised co-operative family business. Participants were concerned with creating varied employment.
Project Area Two Most participants had well planned routine days at work, seeing family tradition being associated with business. Only half of the participants had specifically predictable associations with customs and conventions relating to other peoples' jobs. The ideal family business was seen as a shop or hotel.
Project Area Three Work leaves little time for domestic activities. Place of work could be improved; more spacious, light natural colours, creating a more relaxed working atmosphere. If more people did the same job there would be more social intercourse but it would be rather boring. The ideal job/home relationship demanded shorter hours and less routine.
Project Area Four Returns showed detailed plans for needed

improvements at work in space, colour, ventilation, amenities. A more relaxed interactive atmosphere resulting in more efficiency and better social relationships was envisaged. Interest shown in structure of work situations. Association with other jobs varied and archetypal.

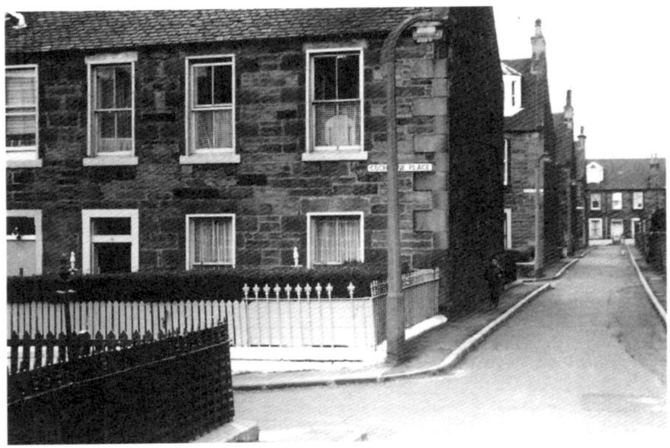

Project area one: Leith

Project area three: Slateford

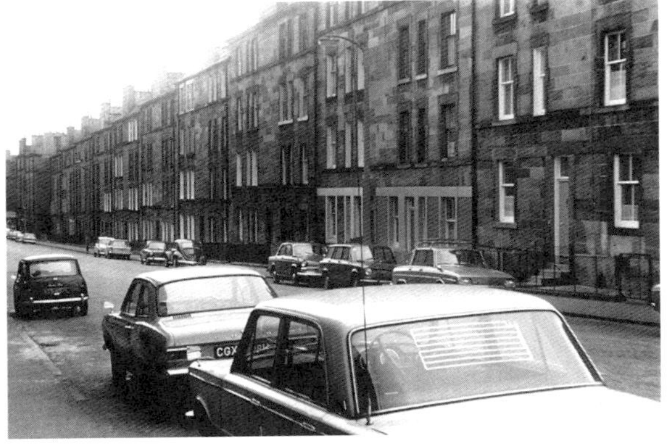

FIGURE 27 Street scenes within the project areas.

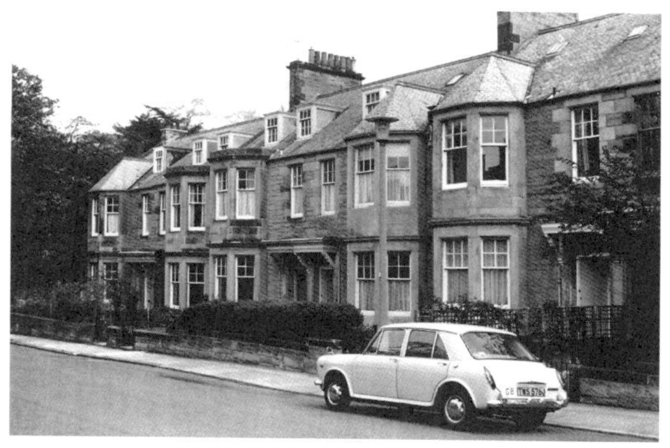

Project area two: Morningside

Project area four: Silverknowes

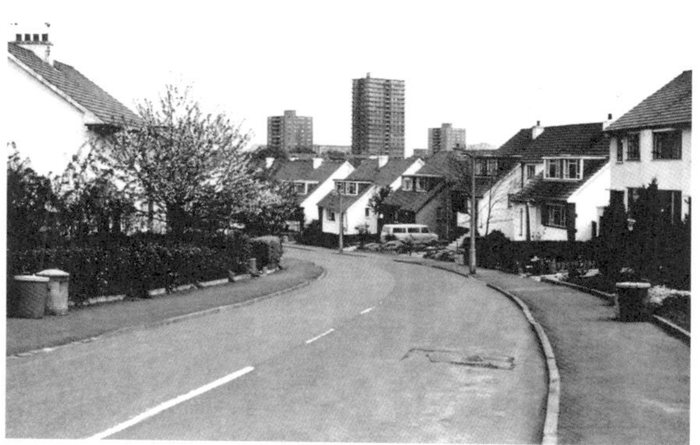

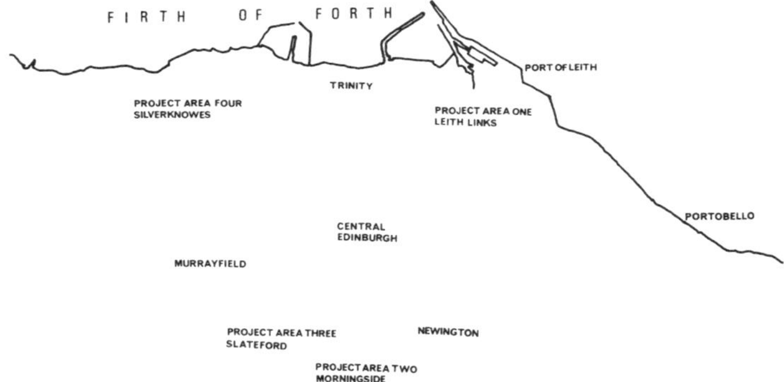

FIGURE 28 Relationship of project areas to each other. Also showing the centre of Edinburgh, location of the central core.

SOCIAL MODEL CONSTRUCTION PROJECT

PROJECT DATES, AUGUST 25th – 31st.

THE SOCIAL MODEL CONSTRUCTION PROJECT IS AN ART WORK THAT ENABLES PEOPLE RESIDENT IN FOUR AREAS OF EDINBURGH TO ARTICULATE THE WAY THEY PERCIEVE AND UNDERSTAND CONVENTIONS THAT DETERMINE PEOPLES RELATIONSHIPS TO EACH OTHER. PARTICIPANTS IN THE PROJECT ARE GIVEN A SERIES OF TASKS WHICH CONSIST OF DEVISING AND RECORDING SOLUTIONS TO PROBLEMS CONCERNED WITH HOW THEY SEE PERSON TO PERSON INTERACTION. THE SOLUTIONS TO THE PROBLEMS ARE FED INTO A COMPUTING SYSTEM THAT FORMULATES NEW PROBLEMS FROM THEM, AND THESE ARE THEN GIVEN TO PARTICIPANTS. THIS LOOP PROCESS OCCURS EACH DAY FOR FIVE DAYS. AS THE BASIS OF THE PROBLEMS USED IN THE PROJECT IS DETERMINED BY THE SOLUTIONS TO PROCEDING ONES IT IS ENVISAGED THAT A LEARNING PROCESS WILL EVOLVE IN A SELF-DETERMINED HIERACHY OF INFORMATION, THE CONTENTS OF WHICH GRADUALLY BECOME MORE MEANINGFUL AND RELEVANT TO PARTICIPANTS AS IT PROGRESSES. PUBLIC MONITORS HAVE BEEN SET UP TO DISPLAY PARTICIPANTS SOLUTIONS TO THE PROBLEMS THEY HAVE BEEN GIVEN. THE NEAREST PUBLIC MONITOR TO THIS PROJECT AREA IS AT_________________________

PROJECT AREA ONE

COCHRANE PLACE.	FINGZIES PLACE.
PARKVALE PLACE.	ELM PLACE.
ROSEVALE PLACE.	NOBLE PLACE.
SUMMERFIELD PLACE.	LINDEAN PLACE.

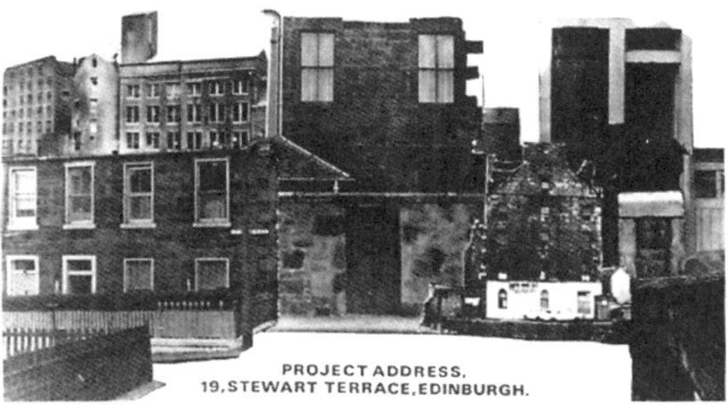

FIGURE 29 Window posters, each one depicting items from the project area that it was designed for.

SOCIAL MODEL CONSTRUCTION PROJECT

PROJECT DATES, AUGUST 25th - 31st.

THE SOCIAL MODEL CONSTRUCTION PROJECT IS AN ART WORK THAT ENABLES PEOPLE RESIDENT IN FOUR AREAS OF EDINBURGH TO ARTICULATE THE WAY THEY PERCIEVE AND UNDERSTAND CONVENTIONS THAT DETERMINE PEOPLES RELATIONSHIPS TO EACH OTHER. PARTICIPANTS IN THE PROJECT ARE GIVEN A SERIES OF TASKS WHICH CONSIST OF DEVISING AND RECORDING SOLUTIONS TO PROBLEMS CONCERNED WITH HOW THEY SEE PERSON TO PERSON INTER-ACTION. THE SOLUTIONS TO THE PROBLEMS ARE FED INTO A COMPUTING SYSTEM THAT FORMULATES NEW PROBLEMS FROM THEM, AND THESE ARE THEN GIVEN TO PARTICIPANTS. THIS LOOP PROCESS OCCURS EACH DAY FOR FIVE DAYS. AS THE BASIS OF THE PROBLEMS USED IN THE PROJECT IS DETERMINED BY THE SOLUTIONS TO PROCEDING ONES IT IS ENVISAGED THAT A LEARNING PROCESS WILL EVOLVE IN A SELF-DETERMINED HIERACHY OF INFORMATION, THE CONTENTS OF WHICH GRADUALLY BECOME MORE MEANINGFUL AND RELEVANT TO PARTICIPANTS AS IT PROGRESSES.
PUBLIC MONITORS HAVE BEEN SET UP TO DISPLAY PARTICIPANTS SOLUTIONS TO THE PROBLEMS THEY HAVE BEEN GIVEN. THE NEAREST PUBLIC MONITOR TO THIS PROJECT AREA IS AT____

PROJECT AREA TWO

WOODBURN TERRACE.	**BRAID AVENUE.**
NILE GROVE.	**CLUNY AVENUE.**
CLUNY TERRACE.	**CLUNY PLACE.**

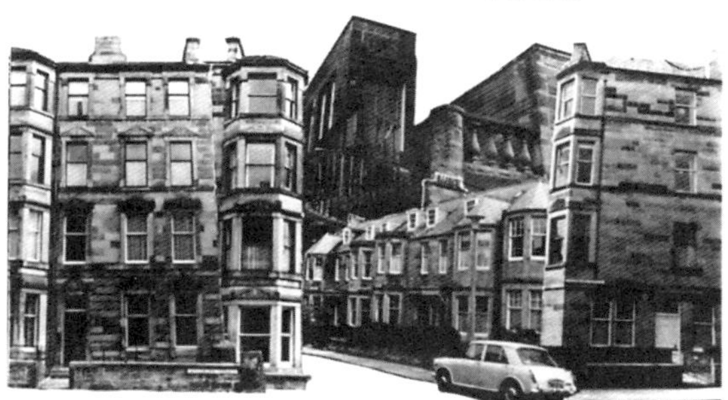

PROJECT ADDRESS, 19 STEWART TERRACE, EDINBURGH.

SOCIAL MODEL CONSTRUCTION PROJECT

PROJECT DATES, AUGUST 25th - 31st.

THE SOCIAL MODEL CONSTRUCTION PROJECT IS AN ART WORK THAT ENABLES PEOPLE RESIDENT IN FOUR AREAS OF EDINBURGH TO ARTICULATE THE WAY THEY PERCIEVE AND UNDERSTAND CONVENTIONS THAT DETERMINE PEOPLES RELATIONSHIPS TO EACH OTHER. PARTICIPANTS IN THE PROJECT ARE GIVEN A SERIES OF TASKS WHICH CONSIST OF DEVISING AND RECORDING SOLUTIONS TO PROBLEMS CONCERNED WITH HOW THEY SEE PERSON TO PERSON INTERACTION. THE SOLUTIONS TO THE PROBLEMS ARE FED INTO A COMPUTING SYSTEM THAT FORMULATES NEW PROBLEMS FROM THEM, AND THESE ARE THEN GIVEN TO PARTICIPANTS. THIS LOOP PROCESS OCCURS EACH DAY FOR FIVE DAYS. AS THE BASIS OF THE PROBLEMS USED IN THE PROJECT IS DETERMINED BY THE SOLUTIONS TO PROCEDING ONES IT IS ENVISAGED THAT A LEARNING PROCESS WILL EVOLVE IN A SELF-DETERMINED HIERACHY OF INFORMATION, THE CONTENTS OF WHICH GRADUALLY BECOME MORE MEANINGFUL AND RELEVANT TO PARTICIPANTS AS IT PROGRESSES. PUBLIC MONITORS HAVE BEEN SET UP TO DISPLAY PARTICIPANTS SOLUTIONS TO THE PROBLEMS THEY HAVE BEEN GIVEN. THE NEAREST PUBLIC MONITOR TO THIS PROJECT AREA IS AT ---------------------------------------

PROJECT AREA THREE

WARDLAW STREET.
WARDLAW TERRACE.
WHEATFIELD STREET.
WARDLAW PLACE.
STEWART TERRACE.
SMITHFIELD STREET.

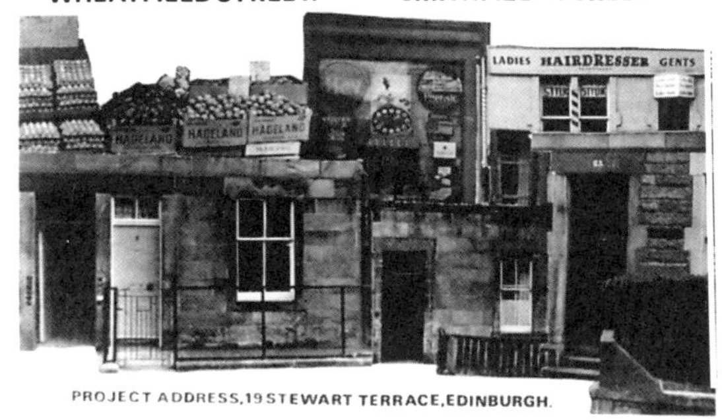

PROJECT ADDRESS, 19 STEWART TERRACE, EDINBURGH.

SOCIAL MODEL CONSTRUCTION PROJECT

PROJECT DATES, AUGUST 25th – 31st.

THE SOCIAL MODEL CONSTRUCTION PROJECT IS AN ART WORK THAT ENABLES PEOPLE RESIDENT IN FOUR AREAS OF EDINBURGH TO ARTICULATE THE WAY THEY PERCIEVE AND UNDERSTAND CONVENTIONS THAT DETERMINE PEOPLES RELATIONSHIPS TO EACH OTHER. PARTICIPANTS IN THE PROJECT ARE GIVEN A SERIES OF TASKS WHICH CONSIST OF DEVISING AND RECORDING SOLUTIONS TO PROBLEMS CONCERNED WITH HOW THEY SEE PERSON TO PERSON INTERACTION. THE SOLUTIONS TO THE PROBLEMS ARE FED INTO A COMPUTING SYSTEM THAT FORMULATES NEW PROBLEMS FROM THEM, AND THESE ARE THEN GIVEN TO PARTICIPANTS. THIS LOOP PROCESS OCCURS EACH DAY FOR FIVE DAYS. AS THE BASIS OF THE PROBLEMS USED IN THE PROJECT IS DETERMINED BY THE SOLUTIONS TO PROCEDING ONES IT IS ENVISAGED THAT A LEARNING PROCESS WILL EVOLVE IN A SELF-DETERMINED HIERACHY OF INFORMATION, THE CONTENTS OF WHICH GRADUALLY BECOME MORE MEANINGFUL AND RELEVANT TO PARTICIPANTS AS IT PROGRESSES.
PUBLIC MONITORS HAVE BEEN SET UP TO DISPLAY PARTICIPANTS SOLUTIONS TO THE PROBLEMS THEY HAVE BEEN GIVEN. THE NEAREST PUBLIC MONITOR TO THIS PROJECT AREA IS AT_____________________________________

PROJECT AREA FOUR

SILVERKNOWES ROAD. SILVERKNOWES PLACE.
SILVERKNOWES GDNS. SILVERKNOWES COURT.
SILVERKNOWES GROVE. SILVERKNOWES BANK.
SILVERKNOWES EASTWAY.

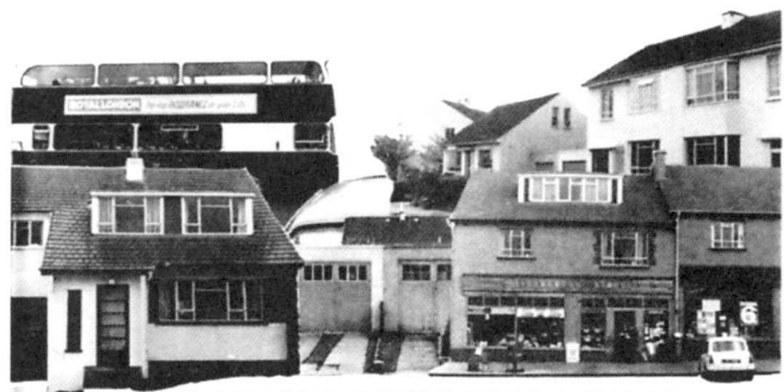

PROJECT ADDRESS, 19 STEWART TERRACE, EDINBUGH.

FIGURE 30 The following pages show examples of completed problem sheets from the four project areas. These have been selected solely because of their suitability for the reproduction process.

SOCIAL MODEL CONSTRUCTION PROJECT

PROBLEM SHEET NO ...r.... **PROJECT AREA** ....1.....

a DESCRIBE THE CUSTOMS OR CONVENTIONS OF A FORMAL SOCIAL OCCASION THAT INVOLVES PEOPLE FROM YOUR NEIGHBOURHOOD AND TAKES PLACE AWAY FROM WHERE YOU LIVE.

a

solution a.

FORMAL OCCASIONS AWAY FROM WHERE
I LIVE ARE MANY & VARIED I
ATTEND THEATRES & RESTAURANTS &
VARIOUS DANCES I AM ALWAYS IN
THE COMPANY OF FRIENDS. SOME LIVE
IN THE AREA SOME DON'T – THERE
ARE NO "CUSTOMS" OR "CONVENTIONS"
BEYOND THE NORMAL STANDARDS
OF GOOD MANNERS.

b HOW WOULD YOU DESCRIBE THE ACTIVITIES OF A CLUB ASSOCIATED WITH THE NEIGHBOURHOODS SHOWN IN BOX A.

Box A.

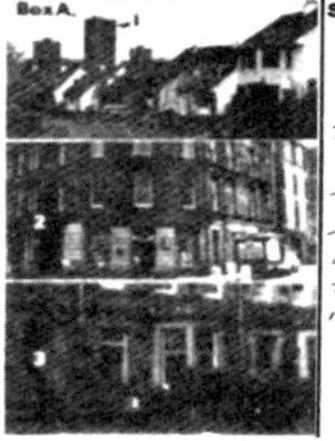

solution b.

A CROSS SECTION OF THE
COMMUNITY LIVES IN EACH AREA.
THEY EACH SEEK RECREATION
ACCORDING TO THEIR TASTES &
TRAVEL TO WHERE THEY FIND IT.
I AM A MEMBER OF A DRAMA GROUP
IN LEITH SOME OF OUR MEMBERS
TRAVEL FROM LIBERTON & CORSTORPHINE
ALTHOUGH MOST LIVE IN OR NEAR LEITH.
WE PERFORM PLAYS OF ALL KINDS.

Project area one

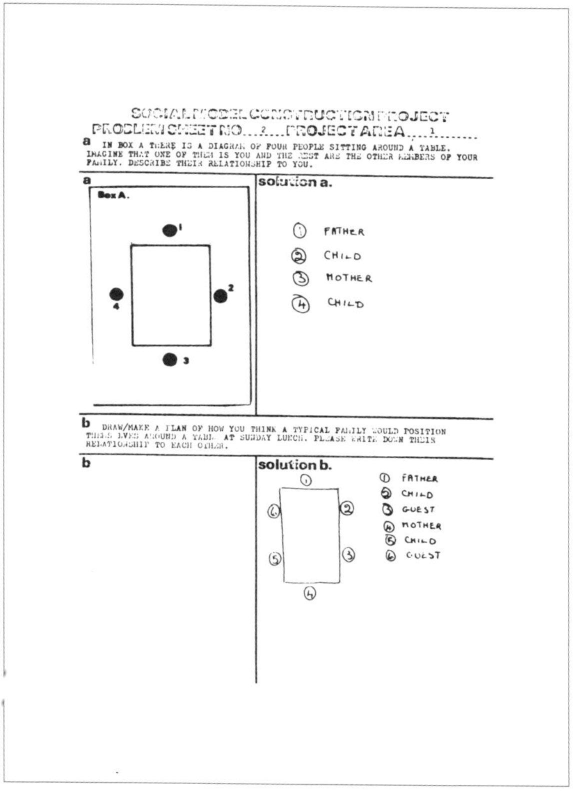

SOCIAL MODEL CONSTRUCTION PROJECT

PROBLEM SHEET NO....2....PROJECT AREA....1........

a IN BOX A THERE IS A DIAGRAM OF FOUR PEOPLE SITTING AROUND A TABLE. IMAGINE THAT ONE OF THEM IS YOU AND THE REST ARE THE OTHER MEMBERS OF YOUR FAMILY. DESCRIBE THEIR RELATIONSHIP TO YOU.

a

Box A.

1 2 3 4

solution a.

1 FATHER
2 CHILD
3 MOTHER
4 CHILD

b DRAW/MAKE A PLAN OF HOW YOU THINK A TYPICAL FAMILY WOULD POSITION THEMSELVES AROUND A TABLE AT SUNDAY LUNCH. PLEASE WRITE DOWN THEIR RELATIONSHIP TO EACH OTHER.

b

solution b.

1 2 3 4 5 6

1 FATHER
2 CHILD
3 GUEST
4 MOTHER
5 CHILD
6 GUEST

SOCIAL MODEL CONSTRUCTION PROJECT

PROBLEM SHEET NO ..13.... **PROJECT AREA** ......1.......
Comparisions from Problem Sheets No's ....10,11,12,..

Project Area One, Most people were happy with their working environment apart from schools. working environments should be more colourful and spacious. This would lead for the most part, cheerful, more relaxed working relationships. Most families would like to run a well organised co-operative family business. Participants were concerned with creating varied employment.

Project Area Two, Most participants had well planned routine days at work, seeing family tradition being associated with business. Only half of the participants had specifically predictable associations with customs and conventions relating to other peoples jobs. The ideal family business was seen as a shop or hotel.

Project Area Three, Work leaves little time for domestic activities. Place of work would be improved more spacious, light natural colours, creating a more relaxed working atmosphere. If more people did the same job there would be more social intercourse but it would be rather boring. The ideal job home relationship demanded shorter hours and less routines

Project Area Four, Returns showed detailed plans for needed improvements at work in space, colour, ventilation, amenities. A more relaxed interactive atmosphere resulting in more efficiency and better social relationships was envisaged. Showed interest in structure of work situations. Associations with other jobs varied and archetypal.

a

a DESCRIBE/DRAW/MAKE A PLAN OF THE HOUSE YOU LIVE IN.

solution a.

UPSTAIRS

FIRST FLOOR

SEMI DETACHED VILLA.

b

b DESCRIBE THE TYPES OF PEOPLE YOU FEEL YOU HAVE A LOT IN COMMON WITH.

solution b.

WORKING CLASS, MEDIUM WAGE GROUP, WITH A PREFERENCE TO A QUIET LIVING

SOCIAL MODEL CONSTRUCTION PROJECT

PROBLEM SHEET NO ......[illegible] **PROJECT AREA** ....[illegible]

a [illegible] A PLAN OF THE IDEAL HOUSING LAYOUT THAT AS YOU SEE AS SERVING YOUR OWN AND GENERAL COMMUNITY NEEDS.

a

solution a.

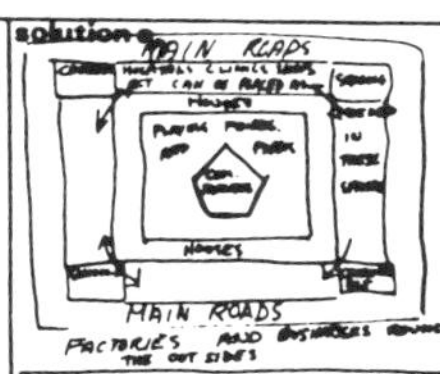

FOOT PATHS AND [illegible] ROAD TO [illegible] COULD BE PLACE AS [illegible] WITH SAFETY IN MIND. HOUSES COULD BE OF [illegible] [illegible] WITH SPECIAL HOUSES FOR THE [illegible] [illegible] AS [illegible] TO [illegible] BLOCKS.

b

SELECT FROM ONE OF THE TWO PICTURES SHOWN IN BOX A THE ONE THAT YOU CAN MOST IDENTIFY WITH, AND THEN DESCRIBE THE POSITION OR ROLE THAT YOU WOULD LIKE TO REACH IN THE GROUP YOU HAVE SELECTED.

Box A.

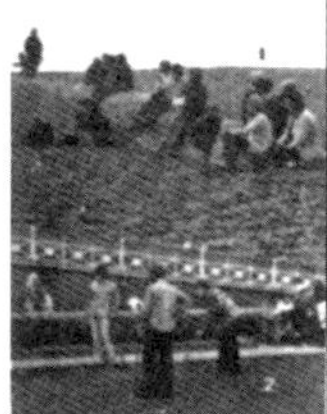

solution b.

SOCIAL MODEL CONSTRUCTION PROJECT

PROBLEM SHEET NO ......[illegible]... **PROJECT AREA** ....[illegible]........

a SELECT [illegible] ONE OF T[illegible] [illegible] A [illegible] YOU CAN [illegible] IDENTIFY WITH, AND TH[illegible] DESCRIBE TH[illegible] POSITION OR ROLE YOU WOULD LIKE TO REACH IN THE GROUP YOU HAVE SELECTED.

Box A.

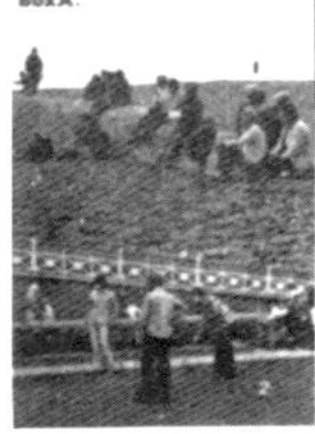

solution a.

I suppose I identify with group no 1 of they are sitting on a beach [illegible], as a family we often spend time there while our children play in the sand I find the end part of the problem totally incomprehensible in relation to my choice of group.

b SELECT ONE OF THE SCENES DEPICTED IN BOX A IN WHICH YOU CAN IMAGINE YOURSELF AS A PARTICIPANT, DESCRIBE THE POSITION OR ROLE YOU WOULD LIKE TO ATTAIN OR COULD SEE YOURSELF HAVING WITHIN THE GROUP.

Box A.

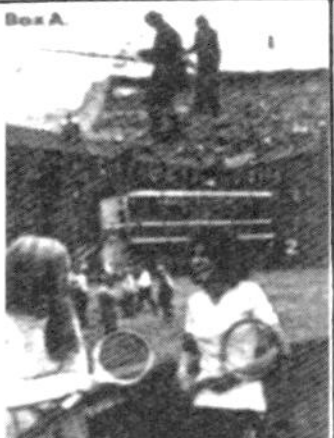

solution b.

I dont fit into any of these categories but I suppose I could imagine being in positio 3 I would like to be treated as a friendly member of the group with minimal desire to win any game.

Project area two

SOCIAL MODEL CONSTRUCTION PROJECT

PROBLEM SHEET NO....1...PROJECT AREA....1........

a IN BOX A THERE IS A FENCE BETWEEN TWO HOUSES. DESCRIBE WHAT YOU THINK COULD BE ITS SOCIAL FUNCTION BETWEEN TWO FAMILIES LIVING ON EITHER SIDE.

box A.

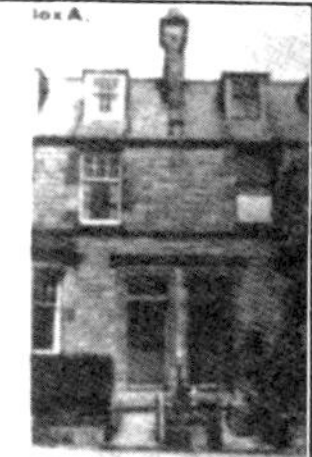

solution a.

It serves as a boundary over which the neighbours may not go, even if almost symbolic. It also prevents children and animals straying so that a modicum of privacy is preserved. When people own a house they like its boundaries clearly marked

b DESCRIBE/DRAW/MAKE A PLAN OF HOW YOU COULD ACHIEVE THE SAME SOLUTION AS YOUR ANSWER TO PROBLEM A WITHOUT THE USE OF A FENCE.

b

solution b.

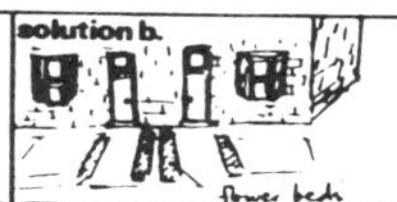

SOCIAL MODEL CONSTRUCTION PROJECT

PROBLEM SHEET NO ...[illegible]... **PROJECT AREA** ....2........

Comparisions from Problem Sheets No's ....10, 11, [illegible]......

Project Area One, Most people were happy with their working environment apart from [illegible], [illegible] environments should be more colourful and spacious. This would lead for the most part, [illegible], more relaxed working relationships. Most feel [illegible] would like to run a well organised co-operative family business. Participants were concerned with creating varied employment.

Project Area Two, Most participants had well planned routine days at work, [illegible] family tradition being associated with business. Only half of the participants had specifically predictable associations with customs and conventions relating to other people's jobs. The ideal family business was seen as a shop or hotel.

Project Area Three, Work leaves little time for domestic activities. Place of work could be improved more spacious, light natural colours, creating a more relaxed working atmosphere. If more people did the same job there would be more social intercourse but it would be rather boring. The ideal job home relationship demanded shorter hours and less routine.

Project Area Four, Returns showed detailed plans for needed improvements at work in space, colour, ventilation, amenities. A more relaxed interactive atmosphere resulting in more efficiency and better social relationships was envisaged. Showed interest in structure of work situations. Associations with other jobs varied and archetypal.

a

a DESCRIBE THE TYPES OF PEOPLE YOU FEEL YOU HAVE A LOT IN COMMON WITH.

solution a. Coming from a family where it was felt that to enter one of the professions was the (or ought to be) the aim in life at the appropriate age – this, in particular being the ambition of my typically Scottish mother for her family – I feel on the same wave length as this professional type of person. Possessing two teachers as sisters, an insurance company owner as brother, a bank manager and a Bachelor of Law as brothers-in-law, to give the background only it can be seen clearly why I am more or less conditioned to think along the same lines as this type of person. I believe these feelings are carried down into members of this type of family's own families. One does not have to explain why one thinks a certain way – the other person instinctively knows, for the simple reason that he or she thinks that way, too. One does not wish to sound patronising or uncharitable, but I think it makes one somewhat impatient or intolerant of people who do not [illegible]

b

b I hope this doesn't sound too awful – I just haven't the [illegible] DESCRIBE WHAT WOULD BE YOUR IDEAL SOCIAL [illegible] moment!

solution b. Despite the impression which possibly is conveyed by the above, I am rather retiring in "social ambition" directions. I prefer to be the person in the background organising and standing back taking great satisfaction in watching everything going smoothly; I prefer it this way.

From a personal angle, a fairly small dinner party in my home or that of a friends whose company I enjoy, with a nice relaxed atmosphere, conversation, discussion, plans for the future in the subject of mutual interest to all of us; this is quite satisfying to me. I am not socially a climber; this is true, not pretence to make an impression. Otherwise, in my hobby relating to canine affairs, any well-run and consequently successful event would be ideal

SOCIAL MODEL CONSTRUCTION PROJECT
PROBLEM SHEET NO...?.... PROJECT AREA.....?.......

a DESCRIBE/MAKE A PLAN OF THE CUSTOMS OR CONVENTIONS THAT TYPIFY SOCIAL RESOURCES USED BY DIFFERENT MEMBERS OF YOUR FAMILY.

a

solution a.

The custom of father's club is that no women should enter except on special occasions and that no shop should be talked. Mother's drama group doesn't have any customs. Children go to dancing class and always have mother to take them.

b DESCRIBE THE FAMILY WHO'S MEMBERS MIGHT USE THE SOCIAL RESOURCE DEPICTED IN BOX A.

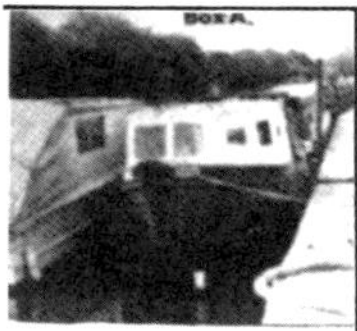

solution b.

The family would probably be middle-class if they could afford to own a boat or perhaps a family of any class who have connection with the sea and boating.

SOCIAL MODEL CONSTRUCTION PROJECT
PROBLEM SHEET NO ...... **PROJECT AREA** ......3......

a SELECT ONE OF THE SCENES DEPICTED IN BOX A AND DESCRIBE HOW YOU THINK YOUR FAMILY WOULD BEHAVE IN THE CIRCUMSTANCES SHOWN.

Box A.

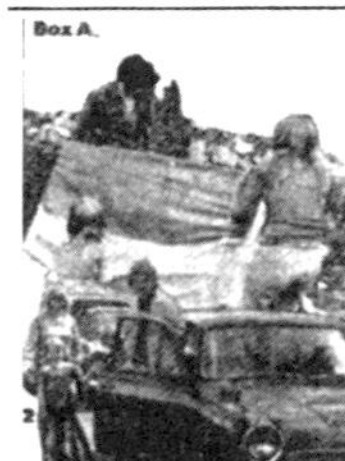

solution a.

If it's a cold windy day and they are not succeeding in putting up the tent, with very bad grace and equally bad temper. If remainder of holiday was cold, windy and wet – ditto above.
If it's a warm sunny and pleasant day and they are succeeding in putting up the tent, with cheerfulness, gaiety and equanimity. Ditto some of weather situation continued for remainder of holiday

b INVENT ROLES FOR THE INDIVIDUALS IN THE GROUP DEPICTED IN THE PHOTOGRAPHS LABELLED 1 AND 2.

Box B.

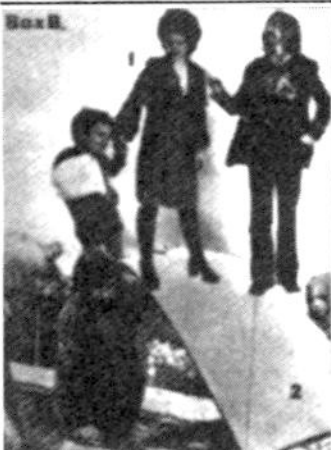

solution b.

1 lady dress designer happily married to architect husband (he might be a photographer or an interior designer or a retired pop star), both of whom dote on their adopted son who broke her arm the other day trying to vault the cabbage patch fence with the handle of an old broom stick.
2/ Father trying to look knowledgeable about the insides of the car when really he hasn't a clue what's wrong. Wife having a sly laugh because she knows he [illegible] all morning [illegible] around with the [illegible]. Daughter [illegible] off because she didn't want to come in the first place

Project area three

SOCIAL MODEL CONSTRUCTION PROJECT
PROBLEM SHEET NO..:.....PROJECT AREA......2.....

a DESCRIBE/TAKE A PLAN OF THE CUSTOMS OR CONVENTIONS THAT TYPIFY SOCIAL RESOURCES USED BY DIFFERENT MEMBERS OF YOUR FAMILY.

a

solution a.

My children play in
the back greens till they get
chased out. when that
happens they go to
~~[illegible]~~ fronts after 6 pm when
the workers are away & play
in there. That's about it
A trip to a library once a week
All in at 8 pm every
night for tea

b DESCRIBE THE FAMILY WHO'S MEMBERS MIGHT USE THE SOCIAL RESOURCE DEPICTED IN BOX A.

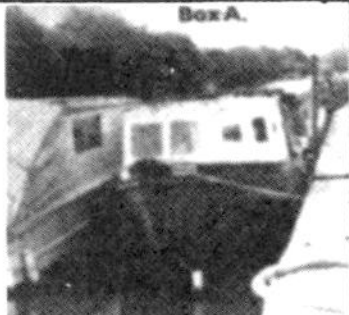

solution b.

I would say an upper class
family maybe live in
Morningside or another
good district go down to
Cramond in the car on
a sunday are members
of the boat club children
if any at good school
go good holidays every year
never know hard up times

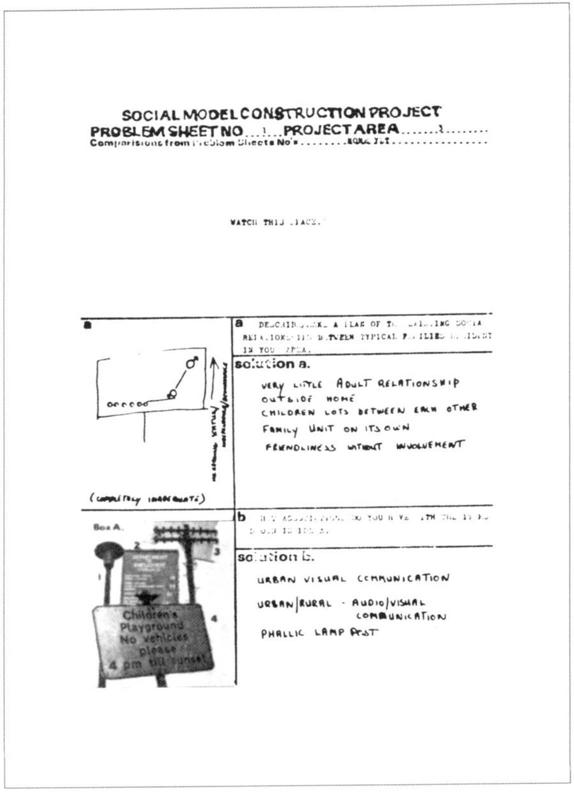

SOCIAL MODEL CONSTRUCTION PROJECT

PROBLEM SHEET NO ...... PROJECT AREA ......

Comparisions from Problem Sheets No's .... [illegible] ....

WATCH THIS SPACE.

a DESCRIBE/MAKE A PLAN OF THE [illegible] SOCIAL RELATIONSHIPS BETWEEN TYPICAL FAMILIES RESIDENT IN YOUR AREA.

solution a.

VERY LITTLE ADULT RELATIONSHIP OUTSIDE HOME

CHILDREN LOTS BETWEEN EACH OTHER

FAMILY UNIT ON ITS OWN

FRIENDLINESS WITHOUT INVOLVEMENT

(COMPLETELY INADEQUATE)

b [illegible]

solution b.

URBAN VISUAL COMMUNICATION

URBAN/RURAL - AUDIO/VISUAL COMMUNICATION

PHALLIC LAMP POST

SOCIAL MODEL CONSTRUCTION PROJECT

PROBLEM SHEET NO .... PROJECT AREA ....

Comparisions from Problem Sheets No's .... 10, ...

Project Area One. Most people were happy with their working environment apart from schools, working environments should be more colourful and spacious. This would lead for the most part, cheerful, more relaxed working relationships. Most families would like to run a well organised co-operative family business. Participants were concerned with creating varied employment.

Project Area Two. Most participants had well planned routine days at work, seeing family tradition being associated with business. Only half of the participants had specifically predictable associations with customs and conventions relating to other peoples jobs. The ideal family business was seen as a shop or hotel.

Project Area Three. Work leaves little time for domestic activities. Place of work could be improved more spacious, light natural colours, creating a more relaxed working atmosphere. If more people did the same job there would be more social intercourse but it would be rather boring. The ideal job home relationship demanded shorter hours and less routines

Project Area Four. Returns showed detailed plans for needed improvements at work in space, colour, ventilation, amenities. A more relaxed interactive atmosphere result. in more efficiency and better social relationships was envisaged. Showed interest in structure of work situations. Associations with other jobs varied and archetypal.

a

a DESCRIBE THE TYPES OF PEOPLE YOU FEEL YOU HAVE A LOT IN COMMON WITH.

solution a. In as much as I am bringing up my son by myself I have a lot in common with other single parent families in terms of the problems that arise from being in this situation, but if you mean what types of people do I get along with, I've just done a quick mental survey of my friends and acquaintances, and they have such [illegible] backgrounds in terms of class education and [illegible] (and temperament and personality) that I find it difficult to pinpoint any particular types.

b

b [illegible]

solution b. My son who is 1½ years, is constantly involving me with other families, just by showing such uninhibited curiosity towards them. [illegible] St Gardens – Nick takes a fancy to one particular family (3 older children and Mum) toddles over to them, performs a few tricks, applauds himself, and before long we all know each other and will probably meet again.

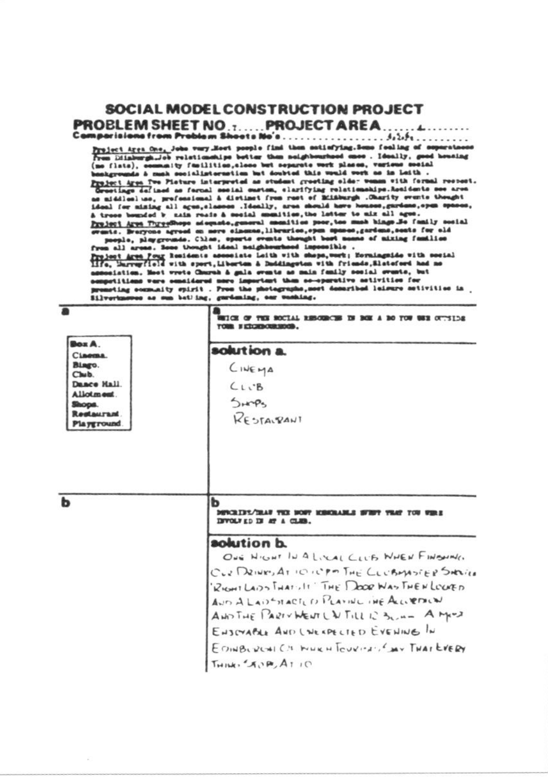

SOCIAL MODEL CONSTRUCTION PROJECT

PROBLEM SHEET NO .7..... **PROJECT AREA** ......4........

Comparisions from Problem Sheets No's .... 4,5,6. ....

Project Area One. Jobs vary. Most people find them satisfying. Some feeling of separateness from Edinburgh. Job relationships better than neighbourhood ones. Ideally, good housing (no flats), community facilities, close but separate work places, various social backgrounds & much socialinteraction but doubted this would work as in Leith.

Project Area Two Picture interpreted as student greeting older woman with formal respect. Greetings defined as formal social custom, clarifying relationships. Residents see area as middleclass, professional & distinct from rest of Edinburgh. Charity events thought ideal for mixing all ages, classes. Ideally, area should have houses, gardens, open spaces, & trees bounded by main roads & social amenities, the latter to mix all ages.

Project Area Three Shops adequate, general amenities poor, too much bingo. No family social events. Everyone agreed on more cinemas, libraries, open spaces, gardens, seats for old people, playgrounds. Clubs, sports events thought best means of mixing families from all areas. Some thought ideal neighbourhood impossible.

Project Area Four Residents associate Leith with shops, work; Morningside with social life, Murrayfield with sport, Liberton & Duddingston with friends, Slateford had no association. Most wrote Church & gala events as main family social events, but competitions were considered more important than co-operative activities for promoting community spirit. From the photographs, most described leisure activities in Silverknowes as sun bathing, gardening, car washing.

a

Box A.
Cinema.
Bingo.
Club.
Dance Hall.
Allotment.
Shops.
Restaurant.
Playground.

a

WHICH OF THE SOCIAL RESOURCES IN BOX A DO YOU USE OUTSIDE YOUR NEIGHBOURHOOD.

solution a.

CINEMA
CLUB
SHOPS
RESTAURANT

b

b

DESCRIBE/DRAW THE MOST MEMORABLE EVENT THAT YOU WERE INVOLVED IN AT A CLUB.

solution b.

ONE NIGHT IN A LOCAL CLUB WHEN FINISHING OUR DRINKS AT 10.10 PM THE CLUBMASTER SHOUTED 'RIGHT LADS THAT'S IT' THE DOOR WAS THEN LOCKED AND A LAD STARTED PLAYING THE ACCORDION AND THE PARTY WENT ON TILL 12.30 AM — A MOST ENJOYABLE AND UNEXPECTED EVENING IN EDINBURGH ON WHICH TOURISTS SAY THAT EVERY THING STOPS AT 10

SOCIAL MODEL CONSTRUCTION PROJECT
PROBLEM SHEET NO. ..1A.. PROJECT AREA ..4..........

a [illegible]

a

solution a.
The Area I Stay In Has Much To Recommend It And The Only Change I Would Make Is As Below

In This Way Cars Are Kept Out Of The Area Except For Garage Access. And A Great Deal More Privacy Is Obtained At A Lower Cost Than Normal Designs.

b [illegible]

b

solution b.
A Neighbourhood Which Is Ideally With A High Amount Of Local Pride And Interaction Between Local Dances, Church Functions Etc. I Feel That Activities Should Build Community Spirit And Give People A Part In That Community

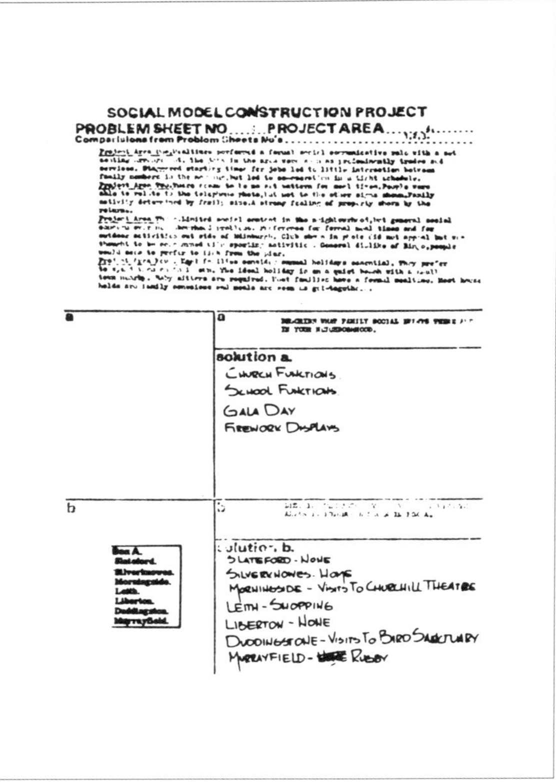

SOCIAL MODEL CONSTRUCTION PROJECT

PROBLEM SHEET NO .... PROJECT AREA ....

Conclusions from Problem Sheets No's ....

Project Area One. Mealtimes performed a formal social communicative role with a set seating arrangement. The jobs in the area were seen as predominantly trades and services. Staggered starting times for jobs led to little interaction between family members in the morning, but led to conversation in a tight schedule.

Project Area Two. There seems to be no set pattern for meal times. People were able to relate to the telephone photo, but not to the other signs shown. Family activity determined by family size. A strong feeling of property shown by the returns.

Project Area Three. Limited social contact in the neighbourhood, but general social [illegible] problems. Preference for formal meal times and for outdoor activities out side of Edinburgh. Club shown in photo did not appeal but was thought to be concerned with sporting activities. General dislike of Bingo, people would seem to prefer to fish from the pier.

Project Area Four. Most families consider annual holidays essential. They prefer to spend [illegible] them. The ideal holiday is on a quiet beach with a small town nearby. Baby sitters are required. Most families have a formal mealtime. Most households are family conscious and meals are seen as get-togethers.

a

a DESCRIBE WHAT FAMILY SOCIAL EVENTS THERE ARE IN YOUR NEIGHBOURHOOD.

solution a.

CHURCH FUNCTIONS
SCHOOL FUNCTIONS
GALA DAY
FIREWORK DISPLAYS

b

Box A.
Slateford.
Silverknowes.
Morningside.
Leith.
Liberton.
Duddingston.
Murrayfield.

b [illegible] IN YOUR AREA.

solution b.

SLATEFORD - NONE
SILVERKNOWES. NONE
MORNINGSIDE - VISITS TO CHURCHILL THEATRE
LEITH - SHOPPING
LIBERTON - NONE
DUDDINGSTONE - VISITS TO BIRD SANCTUARY
MURRAYFIELD - RUGBY

Project area four

SOCIAL MODEL CONSTRUCTION PROJECT

PROBLEM SHEET NO ...... PROJECT AREA ...... 4.

Comparisions from Problem Sheets No's ...... 10,U......

Project Area One, Most people were happy with their working environment apart from schools, working environments should be more colourful and spacious. This would lead for the most part, cheerful, more relaxed working relationships. Most families would like to run a well organised co-operative family business. Participants were concerned with creating varied employment.

Project Area Two, Most participants had well planned routine days at work, seeing family tradition being associated with business. Only half of the participants had specifically predictable associations with customs and conventions relating to other peoples jobs. The ideal family business was seen as a shop or hotel.

Project Area Three, Work leaves little time for domestic activities. Place of work would be improved more spacious, light natural colours, creating a more relaxed working atmosphere. If more people did the same job there would be more social intercourse but it would be rather boring. The ideal job home relationship demanded shorter hours and less routine.

Project Area Four, Returns showed detailed plans for needed improvements at work in space, colour, ventilation, amenities. A more relaxed interactive atmosphere resulting in more efficiency and better social relationships was envisaged. Showed interest in structure of work situations. Associations with other jobs varied and archetypal.

a

a DESCRIBE/DRAW/MAKE A PLAN OF THE HOUSE YOU LIVE IN.

solution a.

b

b DESCRIBE THE EXISTING SOCIAL RELATIONSHIPS ... YOUR NEIGHBOURHOOD AND COMMUNITIES IN EDINBURGH.

solution b.

Many of the younger people go to the sports centre at Meadowbank & to the Commonwealth pool.

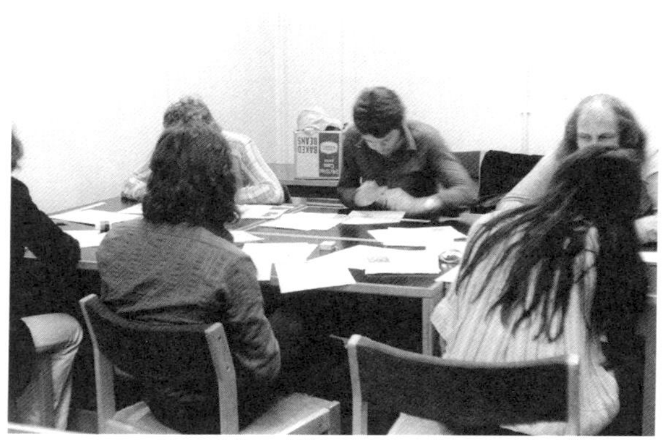

FIGURE 31 One of the central core's committees processing participant returns in the room lent by Edinburgh University's computer centre.

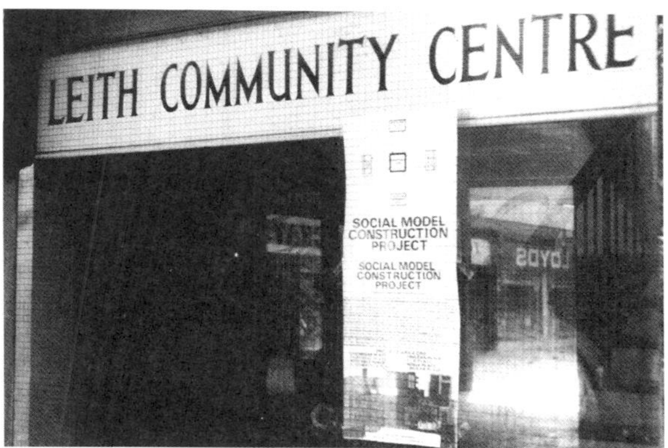

Leith Community Centre

The public monitor board at Leith Community Centre at the start of the project

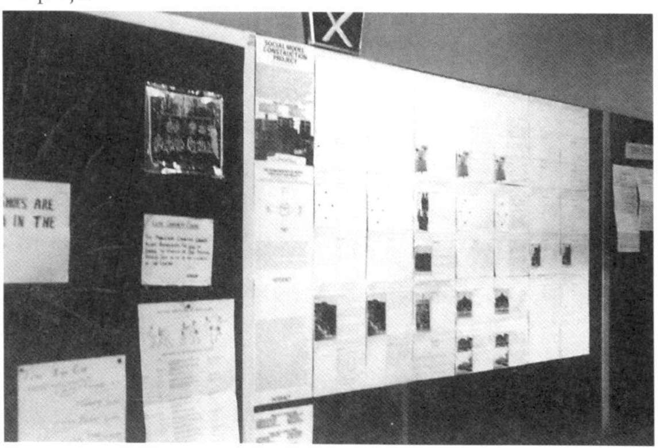

FIGURE 32 Locations for the public monitor boards.

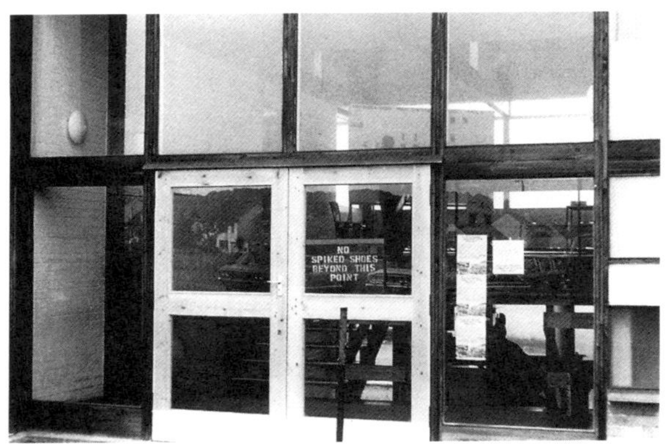

ABOVE Silverknowes Golf Club BELOW The public monitor board at Silverknowes Golf Club at a late stage of the project. The problem sheets formed a file on the board, so that returns could be compared between project states

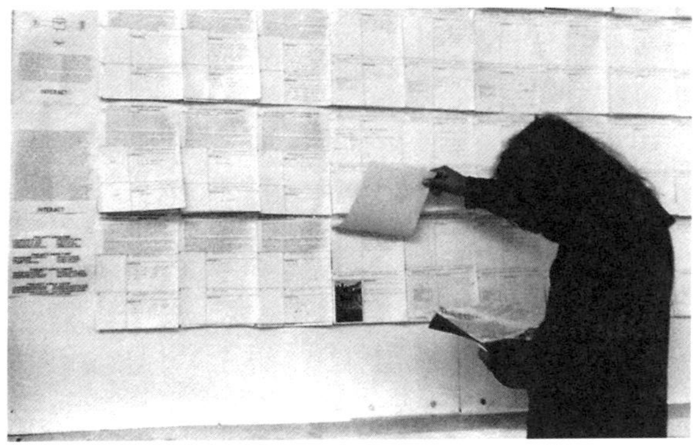

The project in the form described in this Manual is only considered appropriate to the following audience specifications:

1 There is a minimum of two Participant Groups.
2 A Participant Group is made up from the members of a social group that is established within a fixed social, physical location.
3 A Participant Group can be identified as being representative of a social group.
4 Each Participant Group has some distinguishing social characteristics that differentiate them from other Participant Groups.
5 A Participant Group can be linked with a physically compact Project Area that is socially consistent.
6 A Participant Group's Project Area consists of a residential location.
7 Participant Groups' Project Areas are physically separate from each other.
8 All Participant Groups have an existing mental model, or representation, of all other Participant Groups. This can be an intimate or distant model of the other Participant Groups.

FIGURE 6A From the project operators' manual.

meta filter

In March 1973 while the Edinburgh project was being planned, tentative steps were made towards developing a work which would embody much of the project's theoretical background, but would take the form of an interactive machine. After the Edinburgh project had finished, and its implications more fully absorbed, this new work, which was to be called Meta Filter, began to take a more concrete form. A description of Meta Filter is included here as an important development from the two projects just discussed.

intentions of the work

Meta Filter combines methods developed in earlier machine works[30] with those of the projects. Its origins in the Social Model Construction Project can be seen in more ways than one, for not only are the methods similar but so are its intentions. Meta Filter develops relationships between the parameters governing interpersonal behaviour in a group context, and the various codings people use to formalise their social interactions. The work functions by taking the differences in people's perceptions of coding structures back to a common basis out of which the coding behaviours arose. Though the work does not present ideal states, it is seen as a formalised process symbolic of an ideal means of achieving such a state. Instead a state of mutuality is sought, which provides an optimum basis for formalising interpersonal behaviour, though this state is seen as context dependent, and subject to the references of the parties involved in operating the work.

The adoption of a context-dependent standpoint has resulted in Meta Filter employing an interactive learning system, as the means by which its concerns can be made accessible to an audience without them having to obtain special prior knowledge of its references. The work, which physically takes the form shown in figures 34, 35 and 36, is designed to function between two persons who may or may not know each other. A formal interactive structure is established which operating partners use as a neutral tool for externalising what is mutual in their perceptions of interpersonal behaviour. This activity involves the two operators in constructing together both descriptive and prescriptive models, thus reordering the relationship between themselves. In centring the work on interpersonal codings within a group, it is intended that it will increase the operators' awareness of such structures as basic elements within any human organisation, from which they can make analogous inferences to other coding situations. Thus the work functions on two interconnected levels involving both the general perceptions the operators have of group behaviour, and more specifically the relationship established between themselves when constructing a joint model of their perceptions.

description of the work's functions

Interactions between the two operators are initiated and structured by a learning system which presents both parties with the same set of problems concerning how they perceive a symbolically coded group of eight people used as a reference group. This group is presented on a series of 60 slides depicting a series of ambiguous scenes representing everyday situations projected on to a screen positioned in front of each operator (see figure 36). Each one of these scenes is intended to represent a different group formation, within one of five kinds of internal group behaviour (see figure 39 for the full list). Each of the scenes depicting the symbolic group is related to two short statements made by two groups of people representing two different outlooks. These two groups (called group one and group two) were shown the slides of the symbolic group during the construction of the work; each group's collective perceptions of the situations depicted were recorded. The two statements are used to provide two fundamental perceptions which, together with the scene they describe, can be used as subject material for a problem to refer to: they form the problem environment The problems are framed as in other projects, in the form of questions concerning different aspects of the operator's perceptions of the slides and statements. Typical examples of problems are reproduced in figure 37.

As the phrasing of the problems shows, reference is made to a thesaurus, which is to be used in making a solution. This thesaurus has been specially designed for Meta Filter, and consists of lists of words that describe behaviour states, and people's perceptions of the characteristics of other people. The words in the thesaurus are in five sections, each one associated with one of the categories of basic group behaviour mentioned earlier. In response to a problem, the operator selects what he considers to be an appropriate word from one of the lists in the thesaurus. He communicates his selection to the other operator by entering on a keyboard a number given to each word, which then appears on a small display positioned on both sides of Meta Filter. When both operators have communicated their individual solutions to a particular problem to each other, they then attempt to generate alternative numbers through choosing words, to try and reach a mutual agreement by searching for common factors in their solutions.

Both operators are given six attempts each to reach mutual solution – if they have not done so by then it is considered unlikely that they will do so afterwards. If agreement cannot be found the machine then selects another problem retaining the same information as the previous one, but changing the behaviour category. In other words it looks at the same problem area from a different viewpoint. If however they do arrive at a mutually agreed solution, they add an element to their model, and the machine takes the section of the thesaurus that the final word came from as the basis for the next problem.

The thesaurus, problems and statements from groups one and two are all contained within a book called the problem book. Each operator uses the problem book to record his personal involvement with Meta Filter, by making notes of words that have been chosen by both parties as solutions. Each page of problems (see figure 37) represents one column in the matrix reproduced in figure 39, so if agreement is reached both operators progress to a new page. If however they fail to agree they move to another problem on the same page. As with other projects a sheet of carbon paper between two duplicate pages is used to record entries, and after use an operator retains his problem book, while depositing the top entries of his solutions in a box on the side of Meta Filter. The deposited entries are then collected and displayed on screens surrounding Meta Filter to provide a documentation of past operator responses.

considerations arising from meta filter

Meta Filter is an artwork which is context dependent and in this respect it is similar to the projects described earlier. Meta Filter depends on its context in quite a different way however, for instead of referring to the participants/operators' world, the work is neutral and their own reference worlds are brought to bear on it, giving it their particular loading. People do this by the words they choose from the thesaurus, and by the interpretation they give to them. As a result the potential composition of operators is considerably widened, for the work does not presume that any particular world of references is preferable; indeed two quite different worlds can be represented on each side of Meta Filter. Thus the work is open enough for it to function without prespecified operators.

Operators representing different coding worlds, who were strangers before using the machine, were readily able to communicate and reach states of agreement. While using Meta Filter operators are unable to see each other, and theoretically can only communicate through the provided structure. In practice, operators quickly start talking to each other about their responses to problems. The average length of time taken by two operators to reach the end of the sequence of problems is two hours, resulting in a limitation to the number of people able to participate during a set period. This poses an interesting problem, which changes potential operators' relationship to the context in which the work is set up. When considering setting up the work in public, it became apparent that participation time would have to be allocated, thus to some extent restricting its public availability. A card was printed (see figure 40), for potential operators to use to book participation time. Meta Filter is easily portable from context to context, its neutrality resulting in it being appropriate to quite diverse contexts. It is intended for a number of different locations – art galleries, libraries and factories. As the work is moved from context to context, and the number of people who have used it grows, so the documentation of past responses will develop. This documentation will not necessarily reflect the physical nature of the contexts where it is set up, but will certainly embody the social values brought to bear on it as a result of participation. There is no restriction on the size of the secondary audience, which is considered to be made up of people who have not operated the machine part of the work, but have viewed the documentation. Thus the size of the secondary audience could be considerably larger than the number of operators.

The first problems present the major hurdle to the operator, for with these he has to learn the rules for participation: he is then free to develop his involvement. Meta Filter has a considerable advantage over the earlier projects, in that people can participate at their own pace. The pictures of the symbolic group present an already coded world, removed from the operators, and thus is easier to use, as an area in which interactions can be centred, than if their coding worlds were used. The symbolic group pictures present operators with a third world in which they can interact without inhibition, in order that they can accede to their own more readily. At the outset the operators are self-contained entities, though as their involvement increases, areas of mutual perception tend to establish themselves. Both parties establish a predictable vocabulary by finding out what words in the thesaurus they are likely to use. The basis of agreement established between the two operators as they progress in the learning system, adding parts to their model, is allowed to level out at whatever is established between them. As a result Meta Filter enables both operators to establish for themselves a meaningful territory of references, which are not subject to externally applied criteria.

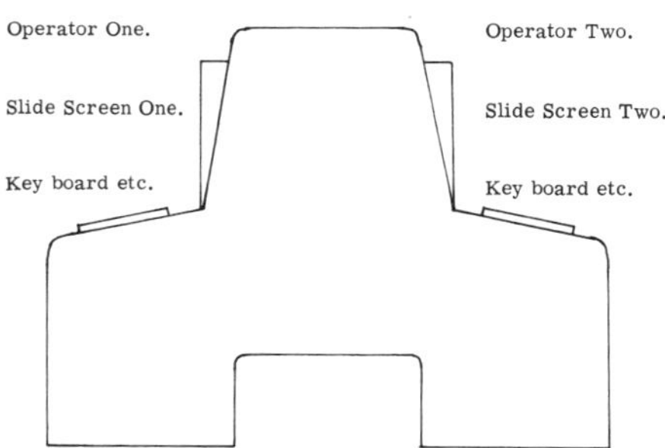

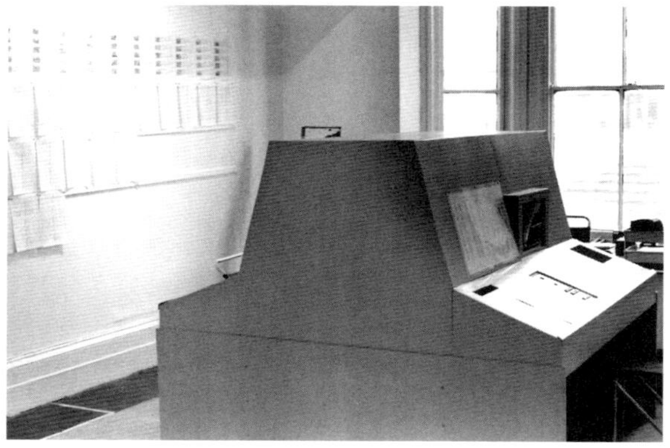

FIGURE 34 Meta Filter, side view.

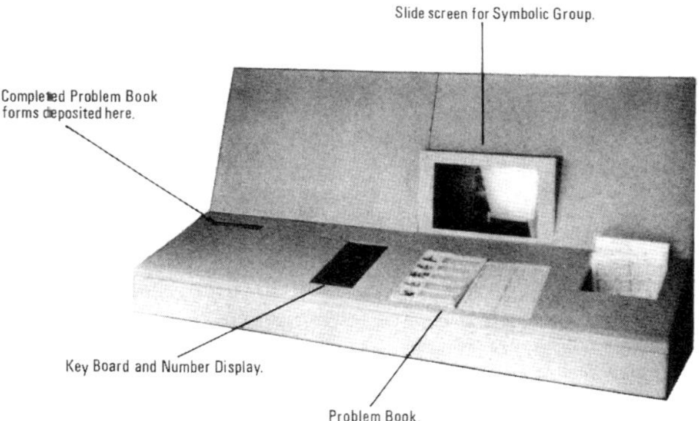

FIGURE 35 One of the two identical sides of Meta Filter. The work is mounted on a stand or table so that operators can sit at either side of it while participating.

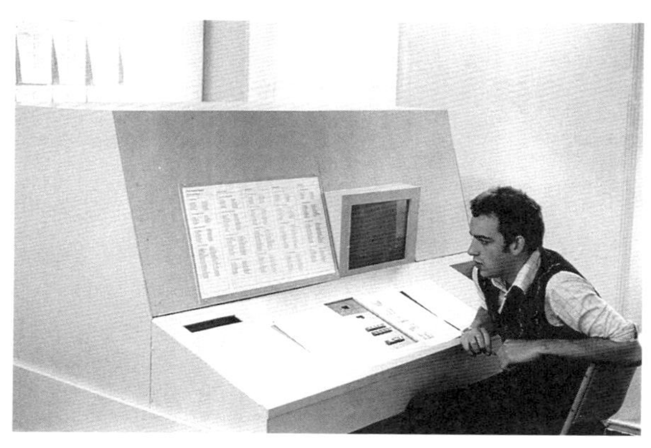

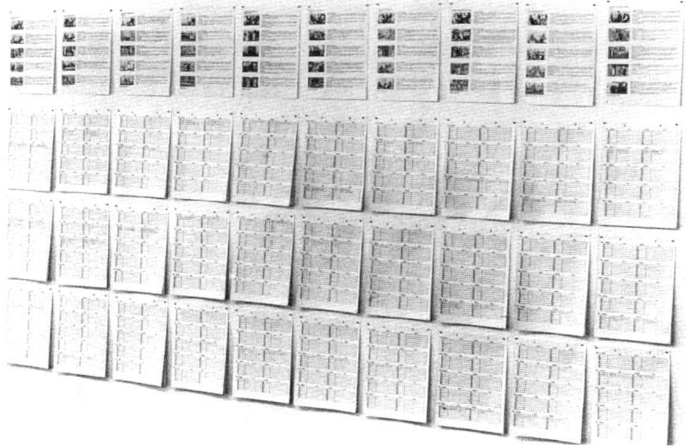

FIGURE 36 Meta Filter displayed at The Gallery, London, in October 1975.

A sub-group's relationship to another sub-group.

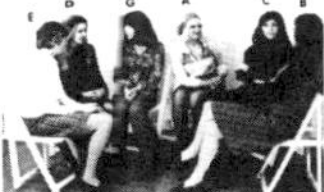

Problem Thirtyone.
The observations by Groups One and Two are two perceptions of the relationships between Persons E, D, and G, and the other members of the group. Using the observations as a basis, complete the sentence below.
Persons E, D, and G, are in a state of.......................... with Persons A, B, and C.
Group One.
There is a them and us relationship between Persons A, B, and C, and the other group. It seems however that they would all be on Christian name terms, and are probably really one group of friends.
Group Two.
The scene depicts one group temporally divided, and thus they would refer to each other on an equal basis.

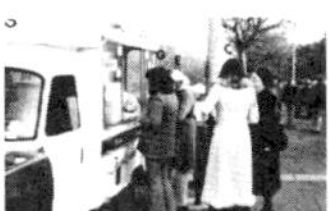

Problem Thirtytwo.
Accepting the observations of Groups One and Two as a description of the ice-cream man's attitude towards the members of the group, select a word from the thesaurus that reverses the situation, and gives the group's perception of the ice-cream man.
Group One.
The person running the ice-cream van would be charming towards the group, and they in turn would be amused.
Group Two.
The person running the ice-cream van would have an agreeable attitude towards the group, considering himself lucky.

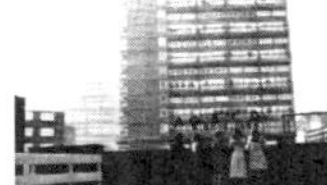

Problem Thirtythree.
All the persons in the depicted group work at the same office. What do you consider might be the outcome of the observations of Groups One and Two on future relations at work between Persons G and E, and other members of the group. Select a word from the thesaurus.
Group One.
Persons A, C, and D would feel sorry for Persons G and E who lived in the flats, but would not say so outwardly.
Group Two.
Persons A, C, and D would show polite interest in Persons G and E's flat, probably would discretely try and find out what their place is like.

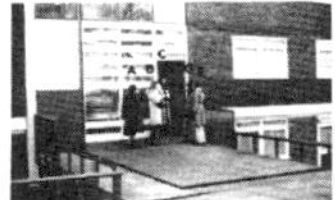

Problem Thirtyfour.
Persons C and D are both residents in the house they are standing outside, and are attempting to impress Persons A and G. Refering to the observations of Groups One and Two as two descriptions of Persons C and D's actions, select a word from the thesaurus that you consider best describes their motives.
Group One.
Persons C and D are pointing out the amenities of their house to the rest of the group, and in so doing are somewhat reticent in order to get the response from them that they want.
Group Two.
Persons C and D are projecting themselves as hostesses to the other members of the group, and are extending an invitation to them.

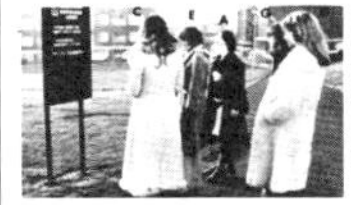

Problem Thirtyfive.
Select a word from the thesaurus that describes what effect the observations by Groups One and Two would have on relationships between the two sub-groups, comprised of Persons A and E, and Persons C, G, and D.
Group One.
The sign implies social regulation, and acts as a provider of directions for conduct. It would have an inhibitory effect on the whole group's behaviour.
Group Two.
The sub-groups appear to be taking notice of authority, and complying with its requests.

FIGURE 37 A page from the problem book. This book is an essential part of Meta Filter's participatory process. Scenes depicting the symbolic group are shown in the column of pictures, next to which are their accompanying problems.

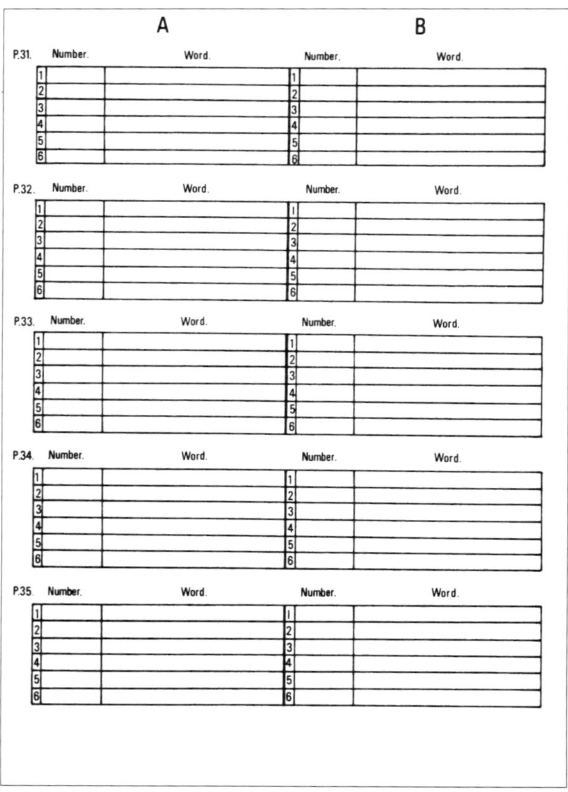

	A		B	
P.31.	Number.	Word.	Number.	Word.
	1		1	
	2		2	
	3		3	
	4		4	
	5		5	
	6		6	
P.32.	Number.	Word.	Number.	Word.
	1		1	
	2		2	
	3		3	
	4		4	
	5		5	
	6		6	
P.33.	Number.	Word.	Number.	Word.
	1		1	
	2		2	
	3		3	
	4		4	
	5		5	
	6		6	
P.34.	Number.	Word.	Number.	Word.
	1		1	
	2		2	
	3		3	
	4		4	
	5		5	
	6		6	
P.35.	Number.	Word.	Number.	Word.
	1		1	
	2		2	
	3		3	
	4		4	
	5		5	
	6		6	

FIGURE 38 This form is used by an operator to record his interactions with his partner.

GROUP FORMATION MATRIX.

Start ↓ (at 1a)

	Institutional behaviour within the group.	Projectional behaviour within the group.	Survival behaviour within the group.	Social provision behaviour within the group.	Reference behaviour within the group.
An individual's relationship to himself.	1e	1d	1c	1b	1a
An individual's relationship to other individuals.	2e	2d	2c	2b	2a
An individual's relationship to a sub-group.	3e	3d	3c	3b	3a
An individual's relationship to a group.	4e	4d	4c	4b	4a
A sub-group's relationship to an individual.	5e	5d	5c	5b	5a
A sub group's relationship to itself.	6e	6d	6c	6b	6a
A sub-group's relationship to other sub-groups.	7e	7d	7c	7b	7a
A sub-group's relationship to a group.	8e	8d	8c	8b	8a
A group's relationship to an individual.	9e	9d	9c	9b	9a
A group's relationship to a sub group.	10e	10d	10c	10b	10a
A group's relationship to itself.	11e	11d	11c	11b	11a
A group's relationship to another group.	12e	12d	12c	12b	12a

FIGURE 39 The conceptual basis of the learning system employed in Meta Filter. Each side of the symbolic group and problem derived its area of attention from the group formation matrix. Agreement between two operators meant they progressed one column.

TIMETABLE	SEPTEMBER		OCTOBER	
MONDAY	22	29	6	13
TUESDAY	23	30	7	14
WEDNESDAY	24	1	8	15
THURSDAY	25	2	9	16
FRIDAY	26	3	10	17
SATURDAY	27	4	11	18

META FILTER

Meta Filter demonstrates how two people can interact to reach a state of agreement, revealing the structures that underly group behaviour and the codes that result therefrom. Problem situations are used in this work to examine social organisation. The work establishes a common territory where the operators bridge the differences in their perceptions.

OPERATION OF THE WORK

Meta Filter is available to be used by two operators, there will be three sessions a day during the exhibition. To participate in operating the work, select a date and a session from those listed, and confirm by telephoning The Gallery; Monday to Saturday, 12pm-6pm.

SESSION 1. 12pm – 2pm
SESSION 2. 2pm – 4pm
SESSION 3. 4pm – 6pm

There will be an initial demonstration of Meta Filter, Tues. 23 September, 6pm - 8pm.

FIGURE 40 The inside of the folded card mailed to potential participants during Meta Filter's exhibition at The Gallery, London, in 1975.

references

1 Motives for engaging in the practice of art tend to determine the particular subgroup that a person joins. Having joined the subgroup, its norms, manifest as attitudes or beliefs, are privately accepted in order to validate membership. The attitudes and opinions of other people help define our social reality; the group to which we belong gives us information on what are correct attitudes. Kiesler-Kiesler (see reference 8) add that not only does the group define correct attitudes, but that the group is a primary source of information relevant to our attitudes. Thus an artist's membership of a subgroup within art's social environment might not only induce pressure to conform to certain attitudes regarding the practice of art, but produce secondary pressures towards other behaviours, such as how one dresses, or where one is seen. These secondary pressures reinforce cohesiveness between members of the group. If for example the motive for engaging in art activities was for the reason of social contact, 'art' would become a means of meeting like-minded people, which would then tend to determine the particular subgroup within art's social environment that the person joined. Evening classes in art at a local institute might be considered a context in which the aforementioned objective might be achieved, in which case in joining the class a person would need to internalise the norms of the group, if acceptance by other members was to been obtained. In such a situation, the art teacher would have acquired and been given special status from other members; his approval would be specially sought.

2 As a means of communication the artwork acts as a transmitter of coded information. The artist encodes the information; the audience, in order to internalise it, acts as a receiver by decoding it. For a fuller analysis of this process, see 'Passive Methods', *Control* Magazine 7, 1973.

3 The effect of contained social conditions on the evolution of language used within its boundaries can be seen in the development of predictive language which is restricted in its usage to a particular defined environment having, as a result of its dependence on special conditions, highly selective associations. This restricted use of language forms a code which has to be learnt or acquired by someone wanting to be understood, or used in communication with members of a group functioning within the particular environment to which it is linked. Such a code has been termed a 'restricted code' by Basil Bernstein, because of its dependency on context. A restricted code can be the means by which a group knows a like-minded person, or demonstrates its differences from other groups. Reference to the work of Basil Bernstein will provide useful analogies for studying the social role of language in art. A paper that I found useful was 'Social Structure, Language and Learning', Basil Bernstein, *Education Research* 3, 1963.

4 The name 'cybernetics' was coined and defined by the mathematician Norbert Wiener in 1947. I provide here two descriptions of the discipline, which outline its basic concerns.

'It was soon discovered that there were certain principles or natural laws governing the behaviour of systems under control, which regardless of the particular form or context of the system, were quite general, and to which scientific expression could be given. Very soon it was realised that control is not a mandatory exercise, in which people are bullied or things coaxed to operate in a desired way. Rather is it a question of coaxing a system towards optimal performance; or, even better, of arranging for the system to regulate itself.' Stafford Beer, *Decision and Control*, John Wiley and Sons Ltd, London

'In practice, Cybernetics cuts across the so-called established sciences such as Physics, Chemistry, Zoology, etc., by abstracting those common features which contribute to an integrated theory of control and communication. The adaptive feature suggests negative feedback as a vital factor, and while this reminds us of servo-systems at one level, it reminds us of human learning in the light of "knowledge of results" at another level.' Professor F H George, *Cybernetics and its Importance for Society*, Monograph 1, Institute of Cybernetics, Brunel University.

5 Donald McKay in his collection of essays, *Information Mechanism and Meaning*, MIT Press, 1972, examines the problem of what is meaningful and meaningless. 'First, what distinguishes the perception of a meaningful object or event from that of a meaningless one? Essentially the first leads or could lead to further inference. To say "X means Y" is to imply that a further representation Y is logically justified given X. Even to say X is meaningful is to imply that some further representational activity is logically justified by X, whether or not the speaker is able to carry it out.' Following this outline of McKay's further, 'X' is subject to the relevance it appears to have to the observer, what Y it infers being a product of the connections made. Y here is the dependent variable and is conditional on what priorities the observer brings to bear on the context in which X is represented: in other words how he chooses, or is able to view it, thus the problem of the perceptual latch when a number of persons witness an accident. They have all witnessed the same event X, but according

to their roles, or degrees of involvement etc., in the accident, so the Y they infer differs considerably, though when they recollect their experiences, they all think their own perception represents the truth. Hence conflicting evidence in the courtroom.

6 'Man from the Twenty First Century' (1971). This grew out of my attempts, while lecturing at Trent Polytechnic, Nottingham, to examine the kinds of strategies and languages the artist might employ to externalise art practice. The examination concentrated on the contextual languages and behavioural routines of two typical social groups resident in Nottingham, knowledge of which I felt would be useful in devising strategies for a future artwork, involving the same or similar social groups. The two areas in Nottingham that were selected are Hyson Green, which is a typical Victorian terraced working-class area; and Bramcote Hills, a new middle-class housing development on the outskirts of Nottingham. Two surveys were devised as an information-retrieval mechanism, one dealing with leisure and shopping habits to see whether they overlapped, the other to ascertain the individual coding structures of the two groups. It was hoped that the first survey might come up with a suitable context to site an artwork, and that the second would provide appropriate languages. Both surveys used a closed question format, the interviewees recording their responses with just a few words or a tick. The procedure was for the questionnaire to be distributed by door-to-door canvassing, and left overnight with the interviewee. The survey on leisure and shopping routines was the first one to be tried, and it was noticed when examining returns that the canvasser who had dressed to typify the person he was interviewing did considerably better than the one who presented himself looking like a student. As a result of the generally low response with the first survey, it was decided to rethink the presentation of the second, taking note of the experience of the student who bothered to relate to the interviewees.

It was considered that by working within the existing references and experiences of the two social groups, a higher response could be achieved. This led to the idea that the second survey should be modelled on a typical neighbourhood advertising strategy which it was felt both groups would have experienced. This led to the conception of 'Man from the Twenty First Century', which was related to the methods employed in films such as those on space travel (*Star Trek*) that use a context remote from the audience's, in order not to inhibit identification with the moralities expressed. The project was never fully realised, but it was to influence later works. It was originally intended that a single interviewer would dress up in a silver spacesuit, and arrive in the streets whose residents were to be interviewed, in a silver time machine. Drawing up outside a house, the man from the twenty-first century was to jump out of his time machine, bound up the garden path, knock on the front door, and when it opened deliver this line: 'I am the man from the twenty-first century, and I have come down to earth in 1971 to ascertain the way in which you perceive your environment', etc. The actual arrival of the man from the twenty-first century was to be preceded by a small poster campaign to create neighbourhood anticipation. The form the project actually took involved five people dressed as the man from the twenty-first century who went to the project areas by public transport. The survey was made up of questions concerning clothes, faces, shapes and colours. The response was over 90 per cent, which was largely attributable to residents enjoying the concept behind the interview, and because it represented something of an event in their neighbourhood. A large proportion of interviewees extended their answers to make elaborate maps, drawings, and writings, and this response subsequently paved the way for the use of open question techniques that would encourage this development in later projects.

7 'The Social Resource Project for Tennis Clubs' took place in

Nottingham during January 1972. The project attempted to centre an artwork on a social resource which was used by communities to maintain social cohesiveness. By changing the way members of four tennis clubs perceived coding structures within the club environment, they could attain a state of mind in which they would examine its relationship to other social structures. The project was to culminate in members of the four tennis clubs re-modelling the game of tennis around their motivations for becoming members. For a majority of club members the game of tennis was not the primary reason for joining, and in some respects it was a rather arbitrary ritual which they engaged in to validate membership. For the first part of the project a specially designed 'tennis club manual' was used to initiate a variation in a member's perception of his club environment. The manual was made up of pictures of objects from the club environment, members' houses etc., with which members would have already made associations. Next to each picture was a question which asked a participant to make associations with the corresponding picture, the questions increasing in their complexity and requiring more involved participation. For example, a typical question was connected with a photograph of a scoreboard. Next to the photograph was a short list of abstract associations, such as performance booster, success monitor. The participant was asked, 'How do you think a scoreboard affects player and spectator behaviour?' The first part of the project involving the manual was considered to be essentially a private activity. However, the next part was meant to initiate public interaction between the club's membership, the main agent in this being the 'I-Spy Book of Tennis'. The I-Spy Book was to be used in conjunction with a series of posters called the 'Tennis Super Girl Posters', displayed in and around the club grounds. There were eight posters in the series, each one displaying a female tennis player and a particular range of items associated with club life, for example, tennis courts, clubhouses, playing equipment etc. The I-Spy Book was made up of incomplete parts of the items displayed on the posters. The participant was asked to recognise the complete item from one of the posters, and record it in his I-Spy Book. A participant then went on to link the selected complete item with another one on a different poster, and then either describe the associations they had with the link, or answer some questions about their choice of linked items. For example, once a participant had found that a complete item in the I-Spy Book was a tennis shoe, he then linked it to one of the clubhouses on the poster of clubhouse items. The participant would then be asked a question concerning the associations he had between the shoe and the clubhouse. The entries in the I-Spy Book were to have formed the basis for a meeting between club members to see how they could have remodelled the game around the priorities expressed. The resulting remodelled game was to have been played in a tournament between the four clubs.

8 Kiesler and Kiesler explore the way in which members of groups acquire attitudes about the group in their book *Conformity*, from which I have reproduced two extracts. *Conformity*, Topics in Social Psychology Series, Addison-Wesley Publishing Company, London, 1970.

9 Gordon Pask, *Physical and Linguistic Evolution of Self Organising Systems*, Systems Research, London.

10 A social resource can be defined as a behaviour routine or physical context that is used by a community to facilitate interactions between its members. The objective of these social interactions can vary though generally it is associated with maintaining the internal structure of a community in a harmonious state.

11 Stafford Beer in his book *Decision and Control* sets out the argument (taking historical perspectives) for management adopting an operation research approach towards decision making. Beer explores the use of various cybernetic models in the practical situation of company decision making.

12 It might be considered that learning theory and advertising research are more goal oriented or deterministic than the concerns of art, in the sense that they are concerned with achieving identifiable changes in behaviour. However, though the goals of art might be thought to be different, the means of achieving communication developed in these disciplines is relevant to the artist attempting to widen the context in which art operates. Dr T Joyce's paper, 'What do we know about how advertising works?' published by J W Thompson, presents a number of models of advertising which attempt to separate analytically the component parts of the communication process. The elements outlined as variables, such as attitudes, needs, attention, recall, etc., are not unique to advertising, and thus useful analogies can be made with problems of communication in art.

13 'At a fundamental level a decision has to be made as to whether the audience is going to be a casual one (in which case it would be undetermined what social group or social environment they belonged to), or a specific one (which can be identified as belonging to a particular social group, etc.). In both cases a model of the audience is important for predicting its responses to the strategies that might be used. In the case of a "casual audience" a model would probably revolve around its commonly shared social behaviour, languages, etc., and in the case of a specific audience, it would be closely linked to the restricted routines, language, rule structure of that group.' Stephen Willats, *The Artist as an Instigator of Changes in Social Cognition and Behaviour*, Gallery House Press, 1972, page 4.

14 Stephen Willats, 'The Construction of Optimum Models in Art Practice', part 3 of 'The Externalisation of Models in Art Practice', *Control* Magazine 8, 1974.

15 Alan Newell and Herbert Simon, *Human Problem Solving*, Prentice Hall, 1972.

16 It is worth listing the options the artist seems to have in using a language that will maximise articulation and understanding on the part of the audience.

A The audience learns the artist's use of language, this being what the artist has traditionally relied on.
B The artist uses common codes or elements of language that are used in the same way by the audience.
C The language of the audience is used.
D The creation of a meta-language which the artist and all participating groups learn and use to describe their individual languages to each other.
E The construction of a meta filter which will encode a message transmitted in the language of one group of people and decode it into the language of the other.

17 Basil Bernstein defines two basic types of codes, elaborated and restricted, which in his paper 'Linguistic Codes, Hesitation Phenomena and Intelligence' are referred to in a linguistic context. However, similar parallels can be made with a visual one. 'Two general types of code can be distinguished: elaborated and restricted. They can be defined, on a linguistic level, in terms of the probability of predicting for any one speaker which structured elements will be used to organise meaning. In the case of an elaborated code, the speaker will select from a relatively extensive range of alternatives and therefore the probability of predicting the pattern of organising

elements is considerably reduced. In the case of a restricted code the number of these alternatives is severely limited, and the probability of predicting the pattern is greatly increased.'

18 An increase in difficulty encountered by a participant in the process of accomplishing sub-learning routines can in itself be generative to him, and this would be especially so when he was anticipating attaining the goal. However, if the composition of the goal varied too radically from the participant's frame of reference, and was presented in its complete form too early in the learning sequence, the gap between the notions embodied in the wider goal and the participant's frame of reference could be too large for him to accept. Such a situation inhibits further involvement.

19 'In a sequence of problems which gradually increase in difficulty, a subject is able to build heuristics from a frame of reference constructed from past experience with previous trial and error procedures, undertaken in providing solutions to problems in the same sequence. The construction of a frame of reference by the subject which is appropriate to a learning routine could be structured to represent the acquisition by him of the artist's intentional concepts which are built into the tasks in the learning sequence.' From Stephen Willats, 'Prescriptions for Task Orientated Methodologies in Constructing Operational Models for Art Practice', *Control* Magazine 7, 1973.

20 Donald McKay, 'What Makes a Question', in *Information, Mechanism and Meaning*, chapter 4, MIT Press, Boston.

21 The West London Social Resource Project started during April 1972, and lasted until the end of the year. After the project had finished a documentation on the methods used formed part of an

exhibition staged at Gallery House, London, during January 1973.

22 As the project did not intend to duplicate in any way the concerns of social science, it was therefore not necessary to adhere to any of its rules when gathering participants. It was not intended to obtain a random sample of persons resident in a project area. Project operators simply went from house to house in the streets that lay within a project area, inviting whoever came to the door to take part.

23 The project's low response in Harrow is curious, for residents were friendly towards project operators when they called round to invite them to participate, and 20 people agreed to participate. When project operators called back for the completed West London Manuals, participants were on the whole apologetic for not doing anything, even though some of them had displayed their window posters. About two thirds suggested that they would still complete the manual, but after a number of visits they still had not completed it, and the numbers who suggested they would diminished with each visit. This project area was therefore reluctantly abandoned. Interest started to wane when participants were given the West London Manual, i.e. their first task. It is therefore reasonable to assume that this might have been the cause. What might have seemed acceptable as a concept during the introductory stages of the project was much less so when participants were asked to carry it through in practice. Perhaps the project, as an operating entity, undermined certain values, such as territorial privacy, that this social group might have felt strongly about, or that they came to feel they did not need the project. However, it is worth bearing in mind that this is all conjecture, and that in other projects, such as the one described in Edinburgh, similar social groupings were involved, and they participated as fully as other social groups.

24 That a project like the West London Social Resource Project was transferable was demonstrated in another project called the Insight Development Project for Oxford. While this was a less ambitious project, it reaffirmed the potential of the problem question, and of the public register board methods developed in the West London Project. The project areas in Oxford were seen as representing typical social groups. The problems in the Oxford project were presented in the Oxford Insight Book, which combined purely descriptive ones with those requiring re-modelling. During participant gathering interviews, people were given a project poster to position in their front window; unlike the West London Project very nearly all were put up straight away. The total number of participants gathered was around 120. The collected returns from the Insight Book were displayed on a register situated in the Museum of Modern Art, Oxford, which was in a central position regarding access from project areas. Most of the participants who completed the Insight Book came and studied the returns displayed on the register. The project took place during October 1972, and was sponsored by the Museum of Modern Art, Oxford.

25 The basic framework for the Edinburgh project was derived from a homeostatic model proposed by Gordon Pask. In his paper, 'The Self Organising System of a Decision Making Group', he proposes an adaptive teaching mechanism which is a direct application of Ashby's 'Selection Amplifier'. In Pask's model subjects form a group acting as sub-controllers, the relationship that they have to each other being determined by an overall controller, through the monitoring of individual subject's performances. Pask links the model with a teaching method 'where the teacher, rather than teaching on his own account, selects students capable of instructing or assisting their fellow students in different subjects.' The teacher acts as an overall controller who determines, on the basis of information monitored to

him, the communication conditions in a group of sub-controllers, in order to maximise the overall measure of learning from the group. Gordon Pask, 'The Self Organising System of a Decision Making Group', Third International Congress on Cybernetics, Association Internationale Cybernetique, 1965.

26 The term 'problem environment', is used in the same sense as 'task environment', as defined by Simon and Newell.

27 'In evolutionary systems, the ability to learn to solve difficult problems usually depends on the opportunities for exposure to sequences of related problems of graded difficulty. We do not expect systems to solve problems efficiently far in advance of the kind they have already worked. Presentation of a graded series of problems provides the opportunity to work up sets of simple heuristics which may later be combined to form more powerful ones. Complex actions are usually formed of previous available elements; blind search through the space of complex methods would be as hopeless as exhaustive search in any other complex domain.' Taken from Dr M L Minsky, 'Some methods of artificial intelligence and heuristic programming', in *Mechanisation of Thought Process*, volume 1, HMSO, 1962.

28 The opportunity to put the theoretical model into practice was provided by the 1973 Edinburgh and Leith Festivals. The Computer Arts Society was forwarding a number of projects under the heading 'Interact' as their contribution to the Edinburgh Festival, and they invited me to participate under the 'Interact' heading. At the same time I was approached by the Leith Festival Committee and invited to contribute to their programme. As Leith is more or less part of Edinburgh, and the two festivals were programmed to run into each other, the two invitations were combined. During its operation the

project had no references connecting it with the Edinburgh Festival, as it was found that residents were somewhat alienated by its tendency to cater for tourists rather than themselves.

29 The audience specifications listed in page one of the project operator's manual were as follows:
1 there is a minimum of two participant groups;
2 a participant group is made up from the members of a social group established within a fixed social, and geographical location;
3 a participant group can be identified as representative of a social group;
4 each participant group has some distinguishing social characteristics that differentiate it from the other participant groups;
5 each group can be linked with a physically compact, socially consistent project area;
6 a participant group's project area consists of a residential location;
7 p;articipants' project areas are physically separate from each other;
8 all participant groups to have an existing mental model, or representation of all other participant groups. This can be an intimate or distant model of the other participant groups.

30 I have been constructing artworks employing learning processes to structure audience behaviour and cognition since the early 1960s. Visual Meta Language Simulation, constructed during 1970/71, represented a key work in the development of my ideas, and is a direct forerunner of Meta Filter. A description of this earlier work is therefore included here. This earlier project centres around the importance of evolving co-operation between two decision organisations – in this case the operators of the simulation – operating within a common problem environment, if both are to succeed in surviving. The project uses a combination of simulation and interactive learning techniques in order to make cognition more

meaningful. The simulation presents the operators with rich connections to a symbolic problem environment, the implications of which are directed at the structure of social organisations. It is assumed that the decision organisations (the operators) have a basic drive to survive, and as a result achieve sub-goal routines related to the major goal of ensuring continual survival. Though initially a competitive relationship between the operators will produce immediate results favouring one or the other, the subsequent increase in problem difficulty means that a threshold point is reached (this varying from operator to operator) where a co-operative relationship has to be established. The simulation increases its difficulty in two ways, one being physical, the other more symbolic:

1 the more successful an operator is at solving the problems on the problem display, the slower appear the decision possibilities on their decision box screen, while the other operator's appear more frequently;
2 as an operator increases his position in the environment by solving the problems on the problem display, part of the environment changes to their colour. At the same time as their position is increased, the mark space ratio between the coloured lamps allocated to each operator alters, the flash becoming shorter for the successful operator and longer for the other. Thus, at the position of dominating the environment with one colour, the flash is too short to see. The problems that the operators have to make decisions about are shown on the problem display and are made up of incomplete shapes (which are a selection of basic codes). When they make a correct decision the incomplete shape fills in, and turns their colour. When a shape on the problem display turns to the operators' colour they know they have been successful; after the complete shape disappears, the display resets to a fresh one. The shapes used in the simulation form the language through which interaction with the problem environment, decision boxes, problem display and the

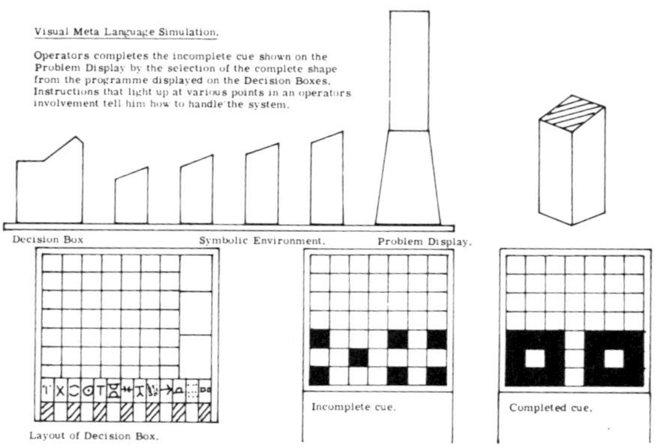

operators is conducted. The project illustrates aspects of social homeostasis in the sense that though both operators start from different base lines, if they are to succeed in surviving a common one has to be found.

From Stephen Willats, 'Simulation Models'. *The Artist as an Instigator of Changes in Social Cognition and Behaviour*, Gallery House Press, 1973, page 16.

Financial assistance was given towards the construction of Meta Filter from The Arts Council of Great Britain, and the Midland Group, Nottingham. This work was constructed with the assistance of Derek Aulton, Electronic Engineer.